Someone So Right

A Godwink story of new beginnings through faith,
even after loss.

Kay Henley Richardson

Spirit Inspired

Copyright © 2024 by Kay Henley Richardson

All rights reserved.

No portion of this book may be reproduced in any form without written permission from the publisher or author, except as permitted by U.S. copyright law.

Published by Spirit Inspired Poetry – www.spiritinspired.com

Trade Paperback ISBN 979-8-9900917-0-2

Ebook ISBN: 979-8-9900917-1-9

All rights reserved. No part of this publication may be reproduced, distributed or transmitted in any form or by any means, including photocopying, recording or other electronic or mechanical methods, without prior written permission of the publisher, except in the case of brief quotations embodied in critical reviews and certain other noncommercial uses permitted by copyright law. For permission contactus@spiritinspired.com.

Editorial Team: Kadesha Powell - KadeshaPowell.com

Acknowledgments

To my Lord and Savior, Jesus Christ, thank you for this life, thank you for this journey
and most importantly, thank you for this season in my life.
In remembrance of my heavenly parents,
who believed their primary purpose in life was to
raise a child that believed in God: Mission Accomplished.
To my husband, Michael, who found me when God knew we would need each other.
Thank you for loving me unconditionally and providing your words for this book.
To my family and friends who have been in my life during all seasons and reasons.
I treasure your love in my heart.
To Susan Hardy, thank you for saying yes to being my prayer partner.
Who would have known the long-term impact of your "yes".
To Dianna Florence, one of the strongest women I know and who encouraged me to pen this story,
I value our friendship more than you could ever know.
Finally to Kadesha Powell, who not only believed in the story but also believed in me and provided patience, guidance and a "push" at the right time to make this book come true - thank you.
I love and appreciate everyone's support, love, prayers and encouragement.
I am grateful that you purchased this book and pray that you are blessed by our story.

Introduction

"For everything, there is a season and a time for every matter under heaven."
Ecclesiastes 3:1

A God-wink is personal experience, sometimes viewed as a coincidence, that is so extraordinary that it is seen as a sign of divine intervention, especially when perceived as the answer to a prayer. [1]

I was the only child of my parents and the only grandchild on both sides of the family. No, I was not spoiled—my mother made sure of that—but I grew up satisfied with all that I had and all that was given to me. I grew up content with being an only child, but that changed as I grew older.

After my father passed, and later on, when my mother also passed, the realization hit me like never before. I had no siblings, never got married, and had no children. Even though I had great relationships with my family and friends, I sometimes felt alone.

This is my God-wink story that shows you cannot look at your situation and give up. God is still on the throne, and He truly answers prayers in His time and in His way at just the right time.

Table of Contents

1.	I Wish I Could See	1
2.	When Your Heart Isn't There	17
3.	I Know Where to Find My Peace	30
4.	Tearing Down the Wall	35
5.	Some One, From God	47
6.	You Please Me	61
7.	I Will Show You Love	76
8.	Didn't Know Who I Am	95
9.	I Love You Even More	98
10.	At Peace	106
11.	Give Her Strength	116
12.	You and I	124
	Conclusion	128
	References	131
	About the Author	133

Chapter One

I Wish I Could See

I Wish I Could See
I wish I could see the things God sees,
The inner parts of man.
I wish I knew my future,
Designed by God's Hands.
I wish I understood
Everything that God knows.
I wish I could be with Him,
And go all the places He goes.
But since I don't and wouldn't know
How to handle what God will do.
My prayer is that Christ guides me,
To do what I should do.
I may be just maturing daily,
Becoming what I am supposed to be.
But Father God, in Jesus's name,
I wish,
Just for a moment,
I could see.
Spirit Inspired™ I Wish I Could See© by Kay Henley

Kayla

January 2019: A Prayer Partner

I need a prayer partner.

The decision was made after a church service. My pastor had preached on "The Power of an Abundant Life,"[1] and his sermon hit home. My pastor reminded me that: *"...the enemy comes to steal, kill, and destroy but Jesus came to give me hope. If I surrender my life to Christ, get under His authority, and put my faith in Jesus, God will shift the circumstances of my life. He will make things change."*[2]

I needed that supernatural change. I was unhappy with work and with life in general. My mother's health was declining, and I had a huge workload with issues on multiple fronts and little appreciation from management. My personal life was nonexistent, and being an only child, never married, and without children at almost sixty, that null and void personal life did not help. I needed a prayer partner who would remind me daily of my identity in God and that circumstances can change even as I turn sixty.

I work out on Saturday mornings with a church group. We prayed before and after walking. During this December meetup, I asked the group to pray for me to find a prayer partner. Sonia immediately volunteered, which was awesome! She is a medical executive in her late 50s and a beautiful and caring person who could relate to my current season in life.

Sonia is divorced and is currently the primary caregiver for her nonagenarian father, whom the Spiritual Walkers refer to as "Papa." She would bring her father to walk with us some Saturdays, and he would share stories about his life with us, going back to the time he worked with Winston Churchill. Papa is a passionate man whose memories are still intact. He reminded me so much of my mother that it was always great to hear his stories.

Since it was a few weeks before Christmas, Sonia and I decided to start our prayer calls on the first Monday in January 2019. Christmas was typical. I usually spent time with family in my hometown of Norfolk, Virginia. Norfolk is a military town located in southeastern Virginia and is about three hours from the DMV (lovingly known as the District, Maryland, and Virginia). At this time in my life, it's only me and my mother. My father passed away on June 4, 1995, after a three-year battle with Alzheimer's and two days after my parents' 40th wedding anniversary.

To say I was a Daddy's girl would be an understatement. I remember as a child when I was mad at my mother one day and asked my father, "Why is Mom around?"

With a warm smile, he replied, "She cooks."

My mother overheard the comment and stated, "We will see who cooks tonight."

The conversation went over my 9-year-old mind, but it didn't matter. He was my heart, and she was his wife who gave birth to me (smile). I had the best parents!

They dated three years before getting married, and I was born three years after their union. My father was old school and worked hard. My mother took care of me, had his dinner ready, and kept a clean house. Neither of my parents had a college degree, but we never felt like we were missing out on anything. My father served in the Army and later worked as a pipefitter at the local military base. He was an old-fashioned husband who took care of all the household expenses, such as the mortgage, car payments, home maintenance, and insurance. My mother worked as a church kindergarten teacher, and my father found her income laughable. So, my mother paid the telephone bill (since she was on it most of the time) and bought her clothes and mine, although my father slipped me some additional "funds" for my wardrobe from time to time. My father was a great example of being a husband, father, and provider, and I wanted one just like him!

Now, after 24 years, it is just me and my mother, and she is becoming more fragile by the day. I headed home for Christmas where did the usual: opened presents and spent the day with her favorite cousins, eating and watching football with family. She loved it, and it was fun for me too. A few days after Christmas, I went on a short trip to Atlanta with another cousin to visit some more cousins, and then it was back to the grind in the DMV.

The DMV is home to a large population of high-income, government professionals and an even larger number of higher-earning private sector employees who support them. I am in the first category since I work for a financial regulatory corporation. I enjoy working with most of my coworkers and love working with all my contractors.

It is a nice place to earn an income. While I feel satisfied with what I do, the lack of appreciation by management, especially the unqualified ones, gets to me sometimes. Explaining to someone two levels up how a project works, only to have them regurgitate what I said to their senior management without giving me credit? *Really!??* Modernized slavery, but I remind myself daily that *God knows what I am doing, and the glory comes from Him.*

As for dating: "For every 100 single, college-educated individuals in the Washington area, women outnumber men 53 to 47. And single women with college degrees are coming here at a faster pace than men in the same demographic, census data shows."[3]

In Prince George's County, Maryland, where I live, the gender ratio is 93 men to 100 women (93:100) or 0.93. This is lower than the Maryland state average of 94 men to 100 women (94:100) or 0.94. The gender ratio is also lower than the national average of 97 men to 100 women (97:100) or 0.97.4. [3] Sounds like good news, right? NOT.

Exclude married men, men who do not prefer women (and women who do not prefer men), men who are incarcerated, men who will never marry because they did it before and/or see that there are plenty of fish in the sea—why even get married?

Then, factor out those available for me. I put a list of my requests on a wall in my prayer closet in January 2018 after watching the movie War Room, starring Priscilla Shirer. The movie had a scene about writing a request and praying for it in a designated prayer room or closet. It was the first time I asked God for a husband. I wish I had received this "brilliant" revelation before I was fifty-eight, but I did it anyway, writing specifically, as the movie said, exactly what I wanted:

-A Christian man who believes Jesus Christ is His Lord and Savior and practices His belief

-Between the ages of 55 to 69

-In great physical shape

-Has grown children and no Baby Mama Drama!

-Retired or has a job and steady income (but does not have to earn as much as I do)

-Loves/loved his parents

-Willing to commit to one woman for life

-I think I have dropped the percentage of available men for me to, say, 1%, but I still pray and keep hope alive.

Myles

January 2019: Life

A little background on my life. Let's begin in 1966.

I was sixteen, and what started out as an ordinary day ended with the day, I would meet my future wife. I was hanging out with my best friend Phillip, and we were making our way to the church grounds.

As we entered the church, beautiful gospel music filled the air. I scanned the familiar faces of the youth choir at practice, but one face was new.

"Who is *SHE?*" I asked Phillip.

"That is my cousin," he said. "Valerie."

I looked at her again, and I was smitten. "Phillip, introduce me to her."

"Okay but be cool. Her mother is watching us," said Phillip.

We walked up to Valerie after choir practice ended. "Val, this is my friend, Myles. Myles, this is Val." "Hi, Myles," said Val with a big smile.

"Hi, Val." I was hoping my voice didn't betray the nervousness I felt inside.

Valerie was beautiful, but there was a huge problem. Her mother saw us talking and sternly walked over. I could imagine what she was thinking as she approached me: "Danger, Will Roger" (referring to the television show Lost in Space circa 1960s).

She looked me up and down and said in no uncertain terms, "Boy, who are you and how old are you? Never mind—if you are with Phillip, I imagine you are around his age. My daughter is thirteen, and you need to stay away from her! She is not even in high school, and she is going to college. Goodbye!"

She stormed out toward the front. "Come on, Valerie!"

Valerie glanced at me. "Nice meeting you, Myles." "Maybe I'll see you around."

"I'd like that," she said as we shared a conspiratorial smile.

"*Valerie!*" Her mother's tone snapped us out of the moment. Valerie hurried over to her mother. I stared after them for a moment. Phillip snapped his fingers in my face. "Earth to Myles."

"I'm going to marry her," I said with confidence. Phillip smirked as we continued our day.

Through Phillip and some family members, Valerie and I saw each other on the side from time to time. Despite what her mother may have thought of me, I made sure to keep things platonic and would never cross a line. I vowed in my heart that I would wait for her.

I graduated from high school and joined the Air Force to avoid being drafted. I spent four years overseas in Turkey before returning to DC. Meanwhile, Valerie graduated from high school and enrolled in Howard University's Registered Nursing program. I wrote to her occasionally while overseas but did not hear back from her. I figured her mother intercepted the letters.

1972

I returned home from Turkey when I was 22. One day I was at 7-Eleven and ran into Phillip. "Myles, welcome back! When did you get home?"

"Hey, man, great to see you!" We shared a brotherly hug. "I got home about a week ago."

"Have you seen Valerie?" Phillip asked. "Does she know you are back? She is not living at home with her mother. She lives in a dorm at Howard University's campus, finishing up her nursing degree. We should go see her."

"Well, I am not sure she wants to see me." I shrugged my shoulders. "She never responded to my letters."

"Man, you know she didn't get those letters," Phillip said. "Mother Superior intercepted them."

"I figured," I said. "Does she have a boyfriend?" "She's engaged."

My heart dropped into my stomach. "What?"

Phillip burst out laughing. "I'm kidding. She's single as far as I know."

"Not funny."

"Let's go over there," he said. "She's not too far from here."

"Now?" A million thoughts ran through my head. Would she like me? Could this be our chance?

"Why not?" Phillip said. "You got something better to do?" "Lead the way."

Phillip and I immediately left 7-Eleven and went to Valerie's dorm room at Howard. She opened the door and invited us in.

She was even more beautiful than I remembered. When she closed the door, she hugged me like I didn't realize how much I needed a hug. After about ten minutes of chatting, Phillip made up some excuse on why he had to leave. It was just me and her at that point.

"Welcome back! How was Turkey?" said Valerie.

"So you knew I was in Turkey. Why did you not respond to any of my letters?" I replied. "My cousin told me you were in Turkey. I never received any letters from you. Oh, you mailed them to my mother's house. I am so sorry. I never received them." "I figured as much," I said. "I never stopped thinking about you."

"Myles, I still love you, and I have missed you so much," she said as she grabbed me and held me tight.

"I love you too," I exclaimed.

We kissed, and from that day on, we were inseparable. That was September 1973. We were married on January 19, 1974.

Valerie became a nurse at Howard University Hospital, and after a stint at a few transitional jobs, I rose the ranks and became a Loan Executive with a local credit union. We had a great marriage; we served in the church, traveled the world, and raised two children—a boy and a girl—who are now successful adults with their own children.

Valerie retired in 2008 due to work-related knee issues from standing on her feet all day.

As a result, she had both of her knees replaced between 2009 and 2010. I joined her in retirement in 2015. We were enjoying family, grandchildren, our church engagements, and traveling with our friends.

Change

Life was good until January 11, 2019. In August 2018, my wife underwent a successful operation to remove cancer in her esophagus. However, in October of the same year, she was recovering from a broken ankle, which left her unable to navigate our stairs.

"Valerie, I am taking you to the hospital. Something's not right," I stated. She had not been feeling well since Christmas.

"I agree, Myles. Let's go."

Valerie spent four days in the hospital. The doctors determined that she had an ulcer and pancreatitis. The doctor prescribed medication and said things should settle down in a few days. She came home on January 15.

I immediately took the prescribed prescriptions to be filled for the following day. The next morning, Valerie said, "Myles, can you help me get out of bed?"

"Sure, Honey," I said. As I helped her up, she passed out in my arms. "Valerie! Please wake up! Baby, please, wake up, PLEASE!"

I shouted and pleaded with her to wake up, but there was no response. I gently laid her back down and called 911.

"911," the voice on the line said, "Please hold." "HOLD! NOOOO!" I yelled to an empty line.

I picked up my cell phone and called 911 again, and once again, I was put on hold. After what seemed like an eternity, probably only two to three minutes, someone finally answered.

I was back in the room and Valerie was still not responding. The operator asked, "What is the emergency?"

"My wife passed out and she will not wake up," I said.

"How long has she been unconscious? Did she slip? Did she eat something that made her pass out?"

"NO! I don't know! I need someone here fast!"

"Paramedics are on their way. Where are you in the house?" "Upstairs bedroom," I replied.

"Please go downstairs and unlock the door so the paramedics can come in. They should be

there shortly. Please keep me on the line until they arrive. Do you know how to administer CPR?"

"NO," I yelled. I felt helpless.

"It's okay. You said your name is Myles, right? Myles, I need you to take a deep breath so I can instruct you on how to administer CPR."

As instructed, I ran downstairs and unlocked the door. I sprinted back upstairs, phone in hand as the operator walked me through the CPR process. Valerie still did not respond.

Within ten minutes the paramedics arrived and came upstairs. They worked on her for about an hour before they told me she was gone.

Valerie died three days before our 45th anniversary.

I called my son and daughter and told them that their mother had transitioned. They immediately came to the house. I cried. I cried by myself, and I cried with my children. This was the first time my children had ever seen me cry.

My children took turns staying with me for a week after the funeral so I wouldn't be alone. "Mikael, Toni, thank you both for being here with me but you both have families and need to go home and be with them," I said. "I need some time to process everything."

"Dad, we understand," said Mikael. "Just call us if you need anything." "We love you, Dad," said Toni as they both left the house.

I was very knowledgeable about the grieving process because Valerie established and initially taught our church's Bereavement Ministry in 1990. She created a six-week grieving program and support group after the death of her mother. It was therapy for her and also benefited the church. The program is currently still taking place at the church. Working with Valerie to create the program provided an in-depth knowledge of the grieving process.

I recognized every emotion and feeling I had from the time of her death. Most importantly, the knowledge obtained from supporting her and attending the classes gave me the emotional sensitivity to know how to grieve. I was not mad at God; I appreciated God for taking the discomfort from my wife. Only God could have prepared me for what I would need in 2019.

Knowing and recognizing the stages of the grieving process helped me get to the acceptance stage a little easier. I did all that I could for my wife while she was living. Now that she was gone, I knew I was left here for some purpose yet to be revealed. By the end of March 2019, I had reached the acceptance stage. I was home alone and in a good place, and although I missed Val, I was at peace with God.

Kayla

January 2019: Dating

Do you know how you make those New Year's Resolutions that you don't keep? Well, I did that too, but I kept the best one: I started the year with a prayer partner. Sonia and I talked every weekday morning between 7:15 and 8:00 before our workday. We recapped what was going on in our lives. I talked about work, my mother's declining health, and my non-dating life, which hopefully was about to change. Sonia began the conversation with updates on her father, work, and her non-dating life. We were perfect for each other!

I also started in January 2019 by setting up a profile on an online dating site. My friends (and I question that status) told me since all I do is work, travel, and go to church, "meeting a man your age" would be challenging. See why I question their friend status? I took their advice anyway and set up a profile (selected male) on a so-called "Christian" dating site. It seemed they forgot to tell the men (and women!) that it was a "Christian" dating site. Although I consider myself an 8 out of 10 in looks, it was interesting to have men (and women) hitting on me on a Christian website! The website's filters definitely did not work! And the conversations and pictures men provided me – no words! I tolerated the process for a few weeks, and after moving beyond the fake guys, I thought I found a nice guy who lived in a nearby city.

The conversation was good. We emailed back and forth and talked on the phone for a few weeks. He used to own several restaurants, but he had to shut them down due to burnout from working 20-hour days, six days a week. He now works as a chef for the government. Our God-focused conversation went well, and we seemed compatible. We kept the conversation going for a few more weeks, which was fine with me, given it was January in the DMV and the weather was cold and icy.

Death of a Cousin

In the last week of January 2019, Sonia shared with me the sad news that her cousin had passed away. The funeral took place at the beginning of the last week in January, but due to so many things going on in her life, she missed the funeral services. Her cousin had been a member of the church we both attend, and her cousin's husband was still a member of our church, head of the finance committee, and very active in the men's ministries. Her cousin, though, had joined another church two years earlier that her cousin's grandfather founded.

Sonia said her cousin left behind a devoted husband of over forty-four years, two adult children, and three grandchildren. We prayed for her cousin's family and strength for her cousin's husband to move on with his God-given purpose in life. Although I never met her cousin, Sonia was sad, so I supported her through the grieving process.

February 2019: Keep It on the Phone

In the second week of February, I met Chef at a restaurant. Interesting. The brother was visually appealing in his pictures, but I wondered if he knew he was meeting me. Did he just come from gardening in the yard and say, "Hey, I am meeting someone new, but I'll dress like this, so she won't think I'm trying to impress her?"

Appearances should not matter, but sorry, dude, it was our first meeting and first impressions matter. We had shared pictures, and he looked like his photo, but someone forgot to tell this brother that he needed to present himself as a viable option at the first meeting. He looked like a bum. His hair was unkept, the "after-five" look was not working, and apparently neither was his iron!

The conversation was still good, but I was distracted by his appearance (I am definitely not into appearances—at least I thought I wasn't) because it was just too bad. Still, I moved forward into this "whatever." We decided to go to the beach for the Presidential Holiday weekend. Again, great conversation, but appearance, wrinkled clothes, "after-five" facial look…disastrous! We shared the same room, but nothing happened, and I do mean, absolutely NOTHING… not even a kiss.

We talked and hung out the entire weekend like teenagers. We walked on the chilly boardwalk, ate some delicious seafood, and I did some shopping. He mentioned he did not spend money on clothes (SURPRISE!). We chatted some more, but he was definitely in the friend zone for me. This went on for a couple of weeks, but then my mother shut it down.

March 2019: She Is Weaker

In mid-March, Chef went to Norfolk with me for the weekend to celebrate my mother's birthday. Norfolk is close to the beach, and we both shared an appreciation for it. He met my eighty-two-year-old mother.

"He is very nice looking," my mother said, surprisingly in a private moment, "but he dresses like a bum."

"Well, you can't have everything," I said.

While my mother was speaking with Chef, I noticed her appearance. She seemed alert but much thinner than the last time I saw her. We enjoyed church service with her, then headed back to the DMV.

"Your mother is nice, and she is very funny. She does not look her age," Chef remarked. "Yes, she is," I responded. My mind drifted back to my mother's appearance.

We had a great conversation on the way home and agreed that we would remain friends.

Later that day, my mother called when she thought I had arrived home.

"Hi, Kayla, this is your mother," she said. She always announced herself and I never understood why. I am her only child, and this is a direct line, but that was her thing.

"Yes, Mother," I said.

"Kayla, Chef is nice, but you can do better. He must be going through something because the package does not match the content. The content is nice—great personality, conversation, and manners, but he is not presenting it well. You can do better. You waited this long. No need to settle now." She didn't even take a breath.

"Thank you, Mother, for your unsolicited feedback," I said. "I made it home safely, and I am now going to bed. Love you. Good night."

"Love you too, Kayla. Good night, sleep tight, don't let the bed bugs bite," the retired teacher said, bringing a huge smile to my face.

April 2019: They Call Her Mom Rosa

I have several great people assisting my mother with various tasks, such as helping her get out of bed, preparing her meals, driving her to appointments when I am not available, taking her to church, and more. They all call her "Mom Rosa." These young ladies and their families love my mother like she was their own, and I am beyond grateful for that. Even their family and friends love her. My mother is engaging, direct, and does not hold anything back. Her message to everyone is the same: "You need to be saved."

I remember one time when one of the ladies who took care of my mother was dating someone, let's say, an independent businessman, candy-man, bagman—okay... dealer! I came home one evening and the businessman and his bodyguard were at the house.

As I approached the front door to *MY* house, a 6 foot 2, 270-pound man in his 30s, wearing a black hoodie and black pants, attempted to stop me!

"Who are you?" he asked.

"No, who are you and what are you doing outside *MY* house?" I said in a tone not meant to be challenged.

"Oh, you must be Kayla," He replied, moving aside. "You can go in; I'm waiting for my boss."

I brushed past him, thinking, Did he just give me permission to go into MY house? What the hockey sticks.

As I entered my house, I spotted his "Boss," a 5-foot 9 inch, very slim, 20-something man, sitting in my living room and crying.

My wheelchair-bound mother calmly sat next to him, saying,

"Young man, I know you're upset because she wants to leave you, but you need to get your life together first. Go to church and become a legal businessman; obviously, you have good business skills. Fatima would respect and appreciate you." She handed him a tissue.

He wiped his eyes, "Yes, Mom Rosa, I will."

This is a dealer? Punk!

When they left, I thought, *God, thank You for protecting my mother and my good government job security clearance.*

My mother was a natural at giving advice, and people listened. She treated everyone with the same respect, regardless of their background. There was another time when her primary caregiver, Dorothy's brother, Guy, was released from jail and visited her on his second day out of prison.

Unbeknownst to me, my mother had been pen pals with him. As he sat at the dining room, known as the *"table of wisdom and counseling,"* where she held court with everyone who came to the house.

"Young man, you served your time. Don't do nothin' to get you back there." "Yes, Mom Rosa," said Guy.

"And look here, you been in jail for a while, and I am sure you have needs. Go to church, get saved, and wrap that thing up! Don't be going out here getting a bunch of girls pregnant.

Pick one and stick with her!"

Gary did pick one, and after another minor criminal slip, he remembered Mom Rosa's words, turned his life around, became an auto mechanic, and married a doctor.

That is my mother, honest and blunt. She keeps it real with those she interacts with; because of this, those who know her, love her very much. She was a beautiful counselor.

Chapter Two

When Your Heart Isn't There

When Your Heart Isn't There
What do you do when your heart isn't there,
When the things that gave you joy, now make you not care?
What do you do when you can't feel joy,
In people and places in which you seek more?
How do you know what your spirit reveals
When you don't even know how your heart really feels?
When your heart isn't there what do you do?
You stand still...
Stand
.... Until God sees it through. When your heart isn't there...
Spirit Inspired™ When Your Heart Isn't There© by Kay Henley

Myles

April – August 2019

I had taken a one-year leave of absence from church responsibilities to spend more time with my wife during the cancer treatments prior to her death. My cousin's wife, Burt, a fellow member and leader in our church, called me in early April.

"Myles, I got a great opportunity for you. Would you like to represent the church at a Leadership Conference in Florida? A getaway may be good right now. It's paid for."

Let's see, an out-of-state conference, paid for by the church with warm weather. I had been a member for over thirty years, but this was the first conference the church had asked me to attend, let alone represent the church.

A small voice in my spirit whispered, *"You ain't got nothing else to do."*

"Burt, sure," I replied.

Dating is Different

I had been married for almost forty-five years. I was unaware of the current rules for dating. "Wet behind the ears" (if that term is still used) was an understatement. While I was at the conference, I attended as many sessions as I could so that I could bring back a report of all the good information I had obtained. This would let the leaders know that they made the right choice in sending me.

However, even with thousands attending the conference, I felt completely alone. On the last day of the conference, during the final session, I sat beside a woman who we will call

"Mermaid." She was attractive and seemed very nice. During the breaks, we talked. "Mermaid, tell me about yourself," I asked, looking beyond the outside physical appearance, which was extremely appealing to the eyes.

"I have been married twice. The first marriage was a total mistake on my part, but the second one was a total mistake on his part. He even tried to come back. That was not going to happen again. I have two adult children and a grandchild. They all live with me." *Wow, they are adults, and they live with her? Maybe they are trying to save money,* I thought to my naïve self.

"Nice. It must be good to have family close," I responded as I processed the information.

"Honey, they are only there because they are looking for jobs. You know how it is," she answered.

I thought, *I don't know how it is for adults with a grandchild to live with you, but we can defer that conversation to a later date.*

Mermaid lived in Tidewater, Virginia, about three hours from the DMV. I admired her because she said she paid her own way to attend the Florida conference.

"Myles, I am here because I have a calling to be a minister to women who have been divorced. You see, either you are not ready, or they are not ready, but the question is, is God ready for you to be married? That is the ministry I am going to start."

"Nice," I responded, but I could not relate. I had been married to one woman for nearly 45 years, but if this was something she believed God wanted her to do, then who was I to stand in her way?

We talked when we returned to our respective hometowns and began dating in May. I thought she could be the one, but I was so vulnerable and inexperienced with dating. I guess you could say I was a sitting duck: widowed, good-looking Black man, retired, financially secure, in relatively excellent shape. I went to visit her in her hometown and met her children, grandchild, and some of her friends.

"Mom, this is your new man? He is driving a convertible Mercedes. He got money. You should keep this one. He could be husband number four," said her son.

Number four. Did I hear that right?

"He is just joking," Mermaid responded and pushed me out of the room. "We have to go."

Her children were nice, but her home was smaller than she described and there were other adults and children there. I let those concerns go and just enjoyed her company for the weekend. I even attended a service where she gave the sermon. I forgot the message she gave but the congregation seemed to receive it well.

One day Mermaid came to visit me, and being the open person that I am, I introduced her to my children and some close church friends.

It turned out to be an eye-opening experience.

"Dad, how well do you know her?" my son Mikael asked.

"Mikael, I met her a month ago. We are still getting to know each other. Remember, I haven't dated in over 45 years. This is new to me."

"Well, Dad, she is different. Be careful."

I invited Mermaid to my church service one weekend. When she came to visit that weekend, she stayed in my home but in separate rooms. I told her church would begin at 8 am and asked her to meet me downstairs at 7:30 am so we could leave for service. Mermaid came

downstairs in four-inch heels, a short skirt, and cleavage that completely divided the girls. "Myles, do I look good?" Mermaid asked.

"Indeed," I responded, wondering if we were heading to church or a party. Either way, we were NOT going to sit in my usual area. I stalled and we got to church after 8 am. We sat in the upper back section of the sanctuary, away from all who knew me. When service was over, we were the first to leave.

We visited each other until July, but something was not adding up. My children were on top of it, though. One day, while sitting with my children, I felt like something was up. They exchanged looks with each other as if waiting for the other to speak. I left the room as they continued their conversation in hushed whispers.

"Toni," my tech-savvy son said to his sister, "I am checking out that gold digger.

Something is not right. Mermaid is not adding up. Now, she looks good on the outside, but the inside is not adding up. I am checking her out."

"Brother, please do," Toni responded. "I am not feeling her. She sees her meal ticket and it is not going to be my daddy. She told me she wants to marry him! That is not happening on our watch."

Mikael did a background check on Mermaid through social media, court records, and other ways. My son did a good job with his investigation and shared the news with Toni.

"Toni, intervention time. *This woman gots to go!* Sis, she has been married three times, filed bankruptcy twice, and does not own her home or any of her cars. Her credit score is below 500! Daddy doesn't even know what a 500-credit score looks like. One of her husbands is in jail, and one of her children just got out of jail. She has those boobs hanging out all on Facebook, which Dad is not on, so he can't see this. From her post, you can tell she is on the hunt."

"She's definitely not for Daddy," responded Toni. "Family meeting time."

My children approached me and shared all they discovered about her. She had lied to me.

Gullible me—I was not ready to date. Mermaid was coming up that weekend and I confronted her with the information at the door.

"Why did you have your children check me out?" she said. She was HOT and avoided the discussion of the information.

"Want to tell me anything?" I asked.

"That stuff is not true, at least not all of it. My first marriage was kind of annulled, and my second husband, who to me was my first husband, went to jail because he lied to me and his

job about some money that was showing up in his personal account. We got divorced, and my next husband just could not afford the life I deserved. The bankruptcies were not my fault. Those people, "businesses" and "bankers," they got money. I made some bad choices, but they were harassing me. They'll get theirs anyways."

"Interesting," I muttered as I stood by the door, waiting for her to get the message that she had to go.

"Well, since you don't trust me and your children invaded my privacy, I am going home

now," she said and slowly turned away from the door. "No need for me to stay. This is not going to work."

"You are right. I pray for you the best. Drive safely," I replied as I closed the door. *Well, that dating thing didn't work out so well.* I thought as I sat to process.

I decided to focus on serving in the church and leaving the honeys alone. I took the entire family on a summer Alaskan Cruise. I was appreciative of how protective my children were of me.

Thank God for His protection and intervention. I continued to pray for God's direction for companionship, which I desire, but I have no clue how to navigate these new dating waters.

Kayla

April 2019: Surrender to God

I began a 40-day Surrender Fast created by a member of my church. It challenged me to write my prayers to God and completely surrender the issues to Him. I prayed for three things:

1– Healing and peace for my mother

2– A husband

3– Peace for me in however God wants to handle #1 and #2.

The Surrender Fast had a Scripture and Word to focus on for each day. The fast began on the last Monday in April 2019 and ended on the first Saturday in June 2019.

In April, I went home to a church celebration that my mother wanted to attend. She was alert but looking thinner. I spoke with her caretakers, and they said she wasn't eating normally, and they reminded me that sometimes older people lose their appetite.

We attended the Saturday church celebration and Sunday church service. As I prepared to drive back to the DMV, I noticed my mother was slouching in her wheelchair, which concerned me.

"Mom, can you sit up straight?" I asked. "Yes."

She adjusted herself, but it still didn't seem right, so I took her to the hospital. After a two-hour examination, the doctor informed me she had a small bedsore, along with being dehydrated and malnourished. The bedsore came from her sitting in her wheelchair all day; the dehydration I could see, but malnourished? What? The doctor assured me it was common in older adults, like her caregivers had said.

After much fuss from my mother, they released her to go home with certain conditions: she had to eat and drink more fluids to help heal her bedsore. I informed all three of her caregivers what was going on. The hospital had prescribed her medication for the bedsore and provided information on food and nutrition she needed to consume to get stronger and heal the bedsore. I returned to the DMV, back to the grind, back to my house.

Several of my sorority sisters invited me on a June girls' trip to the Fairmont Mayakoba resort in Playa del Carmen, Mexico from June 3–8. I thought about it for a while (I should have prayed about it) and signed up. To say I needed this trip would be an understatement. So, off to Mexico I went!!

May 2019: Weaker

Before the trip, I went to check on my mother in the last week of April. She was still in her right mind, but she was physically getting weaker every day. Her caregiver stated the bedsore seemed to be healing slowly, but I still did not feel comfortable with her situation. I decided to take her back to the hospital (against her will). This time they kept her for three days.

The doctor came into the room before we checked out of the hospital. He looked at her with compassion in his eyes. "I am concerned about the bedsore. I think you need to stay longer so I can make sure it heals."

My mother bucked her eyes, something she did when she was not having it.

"She is not going home. She is going to a rehab center so she can recover from the bedsore and build her strength," I assured him.

I worked with a close friend of the family who is a social worker, and she arranged for my mother to go to a rehabilitation center. One challenge for me was that although it was very nice, it was the same one that my father was in before he passed. I had to trust God, family, and friends who assured me it was the best one in the area.

May – June 2019: Rehabilitation

My mother was in rehabilitation for the month of May 2019. Someone from my family or a caregiver was there every day. I came home every weekend, but the bed sore was not getting better, and she continued to get weaker. My mother was in the hospital on Mother's Day weekend. A lot of my family was in town that weekend, and they dropped by the rehab facility to visit her.

The challenge with the rehab was that it did not just have people with short-term illnesses but also those with long-term illnesses like dementia and Alzheimer's. My father passed from Alzheimer's complications at the same facility. I felt some type of way being back in the same facility.

My mother was aware of this, and other than a few opportunities for fellowship in the common areas when guests came by, she stayed in her room. By the end of the month, the medical funding had run out and she returned home.

Worse Than Expected

I brought my mother home from the rehabilitation center on Wednesday, May 29, 2019. The bedsore was worse than expected. Although she could not feel any pain, the sore was down to her bones. During a home visit, a doctor wanted my mother to go back to the hospital, but she refused. She wanted to be home. I spent the rest of the week with her at her house. Although she was in good spirits, she was still different; she had a sense of peace about her. She didn't talk as much as usual and wanted to just look outside her window, and at me. She was so weak but wanted to be at home.

My trip was still planned for June 4. Part of me wanted to go, but another part wanted to stay with her. I prayed to God not to let anything happen to her *(like going home to be with Him)* until I returned. She and my family encouraged me to go, but I assured them if something changed, I would be back in a heartbeat. God reassured me that He would not let anything happen to her until I returned. I flew to Mexico on Monday, June 3, with my friends.

The Trip

My father passed on Tuesday, June 4, 1995. The date was in the back of my head as I traveled from the BWI airport to Cancun. I had never prayed as much as I did on that trip. I prayed for my mother. I prayed for my family. I prayed for the flight. I even prayed that everything would go well at the office while I was away.

We landed and caught a bus to Playa del Carmen. The Fairmont Mayakoba was simply beautiful. My friends and I toured the place on the first day and went to the beach. On the second day, I decided to sit by the pool and complete the last few chapters in The *40-Day Surrender Fast*. At the beginning and end of the book, the author states you will see a move of God in response to your prayers from this fast, and I was beginning to see that move.

On the second night, I got the call that would change my life forever.

"Kayla. We are taking your mother back to the hospital," Dorothy, the primary caretaker, said with compassion. "The doctors said you need to come home, *now*."

A million thoughts began to race through my mind, and before I could panic, God spoke in my spirit. He reminded me of the passage where Jesus did not immediately return when He was told Lazarus was dead. It reminded me that He promised me He would take care of my mother while I was away. I truly believed Him, but (and God knew it was not a non-trusting "but", that night.

I called the airline, changed my flight, and booked the bus from Playa del Carmen back to the airport. Thursday morning, June 6, I caught a 9 am flight from Cancun to BWI. I picked up my car and drove from Baltimore to Norfolk in less than two hours (a normal three-hour drive), and I arrived at the hospital by 7 pm Thursday night.

One of the caregivers had been staying overnight at the hospital with my mother. My mother was somewhat alert, but she was plugged and wrapped up beyond belief. Her legs were elevated, and she had tubes coming from all parts of her body. An infection from the bed sore had gone through her entire body and was now in her blood system. I stayed at the hospital that night through Sunday.

I went home to Maryland on Sunday to get some fresh clothes (I needed the drive) and drove back to Norfolk that night. I finished the fast on Saturday, June 8, and God kept His promise: Nothing happened to my mother until I returned to Norfolk, including that quick trip home on Sunday.

Monday, June 10, I worked from the hospital as the doctors tried to mentally "reach me" and explain my mother's dire condition. I just could not comprehend. We discussed hospice and palliative forms of care to make her comfortable. On Monday evening my mother asked me to sit beside her bed so she could look at me. I did this for several hours as we watched TV.

That night, I played some soft music and watched as she drifted in and out. While she was asleep, I went to the hospital chapel to talk with God. I told Him that I hated to see her in the state that she was in, and although I don't want her to leave me, it pains me more to see her in that state. I remember telling God that I would be fine because I knew He loved me, and I knew He would help me get through anything that happened.

June 2019: The Fly

When I woke up on Tuesday, June 11, my mother was already awake. We talked for a while, and the doctors and nurses came in for the medical work. Family and friends visited all morning, which gave me time to speak with the doctors and do some work. After a work conference call, one of the doctors had an honest conversation with me.

"Kayla, she will not recover from this, and she wants to go home and die with loved ones around her."

What the "hockey sticks" did he just say to me?

I quickly went to the room to confirm with her, and she shook her head and said, "Yes." I left the room so she would not see me cry. I finished working out the details with the medical support staff when my uncle and his girlfriend walked by the door. His girlfriend mentioned the gurgling noise of death coming from my mother. I lost it. I went to the bathroom to pull myself together, and then I went back to her room. Her caregiver, Pamela, was already there. We were talking with my mother, but then her machine alarms went off. Two nurses rushed into the room.

"Mom, are you okay?" I asked, my heart racing.

She responded in a deep voice, "We are fine."

Who the french fries is "we"?

All of a sudden, the strangest thing happened: a fly flew into her room and landed on her forehead. We were on the fourth floor of a hospital!

As I tried to compose myself, I asked the nurses, "Why is there a fly on her forehead?"

"Flies can smell death," One of them answered.

I ran out of the room to the bathroom, crying the entire way. After I pulled myself together, I retreated to her room.

As soon as I stepped inside, Pamela said, "Kayla, she is gone."

"Where did she go?"

"She passed."

I wailed so loudly in that hospital that I knew they heard me in the entire building. Pamela stayed by my side and started calling my family members.

She contacted Dorothy, one of the other caregivers who hastily came to the hospital. Pamela and I were in the hospital lobby, both crying and in shock when Dorothy stepped out of the elevator. Dorothy went to the room, and Pamela later followed her. I decided not to go back to the room, because to me, my mother wasn't there. I have always been taught that we are spirits stored in shells. Therefore, when we die, our spirits leave the shell. My mother was no longer in that bed. She was with our Lord and Savior Jesus Christ and the rest of our ancestors.

Heavenly Conversation #1

I can just imagine the conversation between God and my Mother when she arrived in Heaven (because I know that my "God-fearing, give it to God, go to church, read the Word" Mother went to Heaven).

The Trinity: My child, welcome to Heaven.

My Mother: Praise the Lord! God, thank you so much! I worshipped You from my childhood until my last breath. Thank You, Jesus, for saving my life! Hallelujah!! Now God, can we do something about that girl, my daughter Kayla?

The Trinity: We knew you were coming. We knew your heart's desire. We have already taken care of it. Go fellowship with your family and ancestors. Welcome home!

My Mother: Praise God!

Chapter Three

I Know Where to Find My Peace

I Know Where to Find My Peace

I know where to find my peace
When trouble around me builds.
It's not in my mind, nor in my power,
It's giving Jesus Christ my will.
I know where to find my comfort,
For my faith and hope is in the Lord.
I seek His direction to the right path
This my Father can afford.
I know where I can relax,
To relieve life's earthly pressure.
For joy and fulfillment,
I go to God. He does not judge by man's measure.
See, I know the secret to living successfully,
And through prayer this is what I seek.
I give my cares to my Savior
I know where to find my peace.
Spirit Inspired™ I Know Where I Find My Peace© by Kay Henley

Kayla

June – July 2019: Finding Peace

After notifying family and friends, I went to the place where I found my peace: the beach. I checked into my oceanfront timeshare, got a drink from the bar, and shut off my phone. I had asked my immediate family to give me a night—a night to cry, a night to thank God for answering my prayer, to cry, to think, to cry, to reflect, to cry, to pray, to relax in God's care. I spent the night with "healing" songs on circular replay, hour after hour, falling asleep to the music.

There, I found a peace that truly passed all understanding. God showed me that He had answered my prayer and I had peace. My mother was no longer in pain and discomfort; she was with God, my father, and all my ancestors. She was still watching over me but from a better platform and with the One who had all the power.

The next day, I met up with Dorothy and Pamela at the house. I arrived before them, walked in, and instantly felt my mother's presence. All I could do was sit in a chair and wait for them to arrive. I was numb. Once the ladies arrived, I realized I had to plan a funeral. *Think, Kayla—what is the next step?*

Fortunately, Dorothy reminded me. "Kayla, you have already taken care of the paperwork for her funeral. You already have her burial plot, and the pastor of her church knows she has passed."

All I had to do was meet with the funeral director and plan the funeral program, but I was still numb.

In 2019, my mother's pastor had preached a lot of homegoing services. A church that touted over 2,000 members during my childhood had overflow for many services and was now under a new pastor. Like myself, my childhood friends had moved on and moved away from the neighborhood. Their parents were dying, and membership was down to about 200 people on a good day. In 2019, Pastor Smith was preaching around two to three funerals every month.

"Kayla, it will be two weeks before I can do the funeral," Pastor Smith said.

"Okay."

I now had two weeks of accepting my new normal, two weeks of accepting grief, and two weeks of being numb. Two weeks when I went through the entire seven stages of grief while trying to figure out the next steps. Those two weeks were needed more than I knew. I spent more time at my beach timeshare and more time with my God. There, I found more peace while God healed my heart and soothed my soul.

Homegoing Service

My parents were married 40 years on June 2, 1995. My father passed on June 4, 1995, two days after their anniversary. My mother had prayed that God would not allow my father to pass on their anniversary, and God did not allow him to pass on that day. Now my mother has passed on June 11, 2019—22 years and a week after my father. Note to myself: seek a beach in June.

The service was held on Thursday, June 20, and was beautiful. My immediate family and friends came in from all over the country. My mother looked beautiful as her body rested in the coffin. The four young ladies who had taken care of her over the past years were all in attendance. I had asked people not to cry (the nerve of me), but there was always one doing the most. Fatima (the one with the "Boss" boyfriend) took it very hard and cried most of the service. Part of me wanted to tell her to "Shut up! That is not your mother! You don't see me crying." But the other part understood; that was her mother for the past ten years.

There were so many loved ones at the funeral. My sorority sisters came out strong, as they knew that as an only child, I saw them all as my sisters. Additionally, many friends and loved ones from my Maryland church, as well as other churches I had attended, and my "adopted parents" from other close friends were all there. Flowers and plants came from my sorority sisters, colleagues from work, and many, many others. The words shared at her service were beautiful. There was so much love for "Mom Rosa" that day, which reflected the love she gave to others.

Numb

After the funeral, I returned to the beach timeshare for a few days and chilled. I had shared with the timeshare staff that my mother had passed, and they allowed me to stay (at cost) for as long as I needed. I was still numb and was going through the motions. My plan was to relax and reflect, so I walked the boardwalk in the morning and just sat around the condo the rest of the time, basically in a daze. God was there, and I had a sense of peace. Three days after the funeral and chilling at the beach, God said, "You will be fine. It's time to go home." I immediately packed my bags, got in my car, and drove back to my DMV home with all the "healing songs" playing throughout the entire ride.

On the drive back, I thought, *I need to do something with my mother's house*. The caregivers had helped me clean out her stuff, but I still needed to decide if I was going to rent or sell the property. It suddenly dawned on me that she had asked me about this in the spring. Dorothy wanted to move into the house. So, I fixed it up, and she rented it. I do not know how she could move into my mother's house, but she later told me it was like my mother was still there, so she talked with her every day. If that worked for her—awesome!

Dr. Celeste Owens (who passed in November 2022) wrote *The 40-Day Surrender Fast* and invited me to a healing retreat in western Maryland the first weekend in July. Her book carried me through my mother's transition. Since I had absolutely nothing else to do, I decided to go. It was an intimate gathering where everyone shared their stories of loss. When it came time for me, I shared my story, and people were shocked, saying, "Your mother passed less than a month ago, and you are not crying? Are you okay?" In my mind, I was thinking, *Why are you all still mourning?* See, for me (I did not say this out loud out of respect), I wasn't mourning because "I honored my mother and father."

My parents raised me as a Christian, and I knew *to be absent from the body meant to be present with the Lord* (2 Corinthians 5:8). I was confident in the fact that both of my parents were with my Lord and Savior Jesus Christ, and I had done all I could to be the best daughter to them. My mother was no longer suffering, so I may have been numb, but I was also content that my mother was at peace. I later understood more clearly from the teaching at the retreat that everyone has their own way of mourning, whether it is the loss of a loved one or a relationship. I also realized this retreat was not for me, so I left during lunch.

In August, my close friend Thelma invited me to spend a week in the Hamptons, New York, with her, her mother, sister, and her sister's family. I was with Thelma when her husband transitioned in March 2017. I see now that God was preparing me for my mother's transition.

The Hamptons are breathtaking, featuring peaceful beaches, great seafood, and quaint shops. Although I was with people who loved me and we were chatting and engaged in various activities, I was still not present. I was grateful that I had my own room in the house to pray, cry, meditate and just exist.

Chapter Four

Tearing Down the Wall

Tearing Down the Wall
It started with one, red, solid, and thick,
To fight all my pain, I added a brick.
When people disappointed me.
When loved ones became sick.
When things didn't go my way,
It wasn't a problem; I added a brick.
I blocked it out of my mind.
I ran away, but then I thought about it,
But it could wait until another day.
It became strong and tall; I could handle it all.
What pain could find me? – Hey, I have a wall.
And you could huff and puff.
But this wall man couldn't bring down.
For it was 10 feet by 10 feet Around and around.
Until God pulled a brick, and now it must fall.
It's okay, Christ has it now,
And He's tearing down the wall.
Spirit Inspired™ Tearing Down the Wall© by Kay Henley

Kayla

September 2019: Let's Go to the Movies – First Encounter

My church is so cool! Another church I used to attend strongly discouraged members from going to the movies because it was a dark place. That pastor believed nothing positive could happen in a dark place, and going on a date to the movies is not really doing anything to build up the relationship, as it was just sitting in a dark place (especially not when movie tickets and food come to almost $50!). To the contrary, my current pastor would rent out the entire movie theater and tell the congregation, "Let's go to the movies!" Now you are going to a Christian movie, and you are going with people of like minds but who still talk to the movie screen when they see something they like or don't like. I love it.

Sonia, my prayer partner, knew I had been going through the motions since I got back to work in July: home, work, home; church on Sundays, home. So, she invited me to join her and her father at the movies on the third Saturday afternoon in September. The church had rented out the theater for Priscilla Shirer's movie, *Overcomer* (prophetic title?). We were seated and just before the movie started, a gentleman walked by.

"Myles, come sit with us," Sonia said. She introduced us by saying, "Kayla, this is my cousin Myles. We prayed for him and his family this past January when his wife passed." (Note: Myles's wife was Sonia's actual cousin and Myles was her cousin-in-love). We exchanged pleasantries and he sat down.

I thought *Dude, you are late! The movie is about to start. Take a seat!* Myles sat on the other side of Sonia, while Sonia sat next to her father, who sat next to me. When the movie was over, Myles left first, and then Sonia, her father, and I left.

Myles

September 2019: The Movies – First Encounter

"Okay, I can sit here and look at the walls," I said to myself. "I ain't got nothing else to do, so I can go to the movies. There will be people there from the church and I only need one seat. Getting out of the house to see a good Christian-based movie will be good for me."

So, I went to the theater, and it was already dark inside. As I was walking to find a single seat, I heard my wife's cousin Sonia call my name.

'Myles," she said. "Hi, there! Are you looking for a seat? You can come sit with me, my father, and my friend Kayla."

"Sure," I replied. It was dark and my only goal was not to step on anyone's

feet as I took my seat.

"Kayla, this is Myles," Sonia introduced. "Myles, this is Kayla."

"Hello, Myles," Kayla said.

"Hello, Kayla," I responded as I took my seat. I got to the theater just in time to avoid all the previews—as planned. As soon as the movie ended, I left. Back home—alone.

Heavenly Conversation #2

The Trinity: "Wow! We know it is going to happen—they are going to connect. But Peter, what seems to be the problem?

Peter: Myles is cautious after the disappointment he experienced from the person he picked, and Kayla is going through the motions because she cannot believe something can finally go right in her life. They both need more time. They will be good for each other.

Kayla

First Friday in October 2019: Second Encounter

My church has a women's conference every fall. I helped by serving in several

ministries, but on this occasion, I assisted the church's bookstore. I was assigned to help female speakers who were promoting and selling their books. As I was serving, a gentleman walked up to the table.

"Hello. My name is Myles, and I am here to assist you with the women vendors who are selling their books."

I thought, *I don't recall asking for assistance,* but what I said was: "Okay." We sat there without talking to each other, waiting for about 15 minutes.

Daniel, the bookstore manager, approached Myles at the table and greeted him with a hug.

"Hi, Daniel, how you doing? How have things been going?" Myles asked as they exchanged pleasantries.

"Things are going well. Have you met Kayla?"

"Well, not really. I have been here 15 minutes, and she hasn't said anything to me!" "I understand. She does not like talking to people or them touching her."

In my mind, I cursed, *What the hockey sticks? What did he just say? Seems like Daniel was implying I was standoffish.*

I protested, "Daniel, that is not true!"

Daniel and Myles gave me a skeptical look as if to say, "Really?"

"Okay, maybe sometimes. Daniel, what exactly would you like us to do? *The master at changing conversations did it again.*

Daniel proceeds to give us our assignments for the next three hours. During downtimes, Myles and I had great conversations. He told me about his family. His wife had recently passed, and he had two grown children and three grandchildren, one of whom he had to pick up from school that day. He mentioned he was retired and loved serving the Lord. We chatted anytime we did not need to assist someone with book sales. Great conversation with a handsome Christian man, and he didn't look like a bum. After a couple of hours, he reminded me that he had to leave to pick up his grandson.

I know this brother is going to ask me for my phone number.

Instead, Myles said, "Nice talking with you. Have a nice day!"

What?!! Really?? "You too," I replied, feeling disappointed.

The hallways at my church are wide and long. As I watched, Myles (didn't get his last name) walked down the hall to the exit, and I noticed he had a walk that could only have been given to him by God. "Go ahead with that sway, my brother", I said to myself.

Then I thought, *Dang! Dude, turn around!*

Turn!

A!

Round!

He didn't. I prayed *God, I want one just like him!*

Myles

First Friday in October 2019: Second Encounter

The leader of the men's ministry said they needed workers to help at the women's conference, so I volunteered. On the third and last day of my volunteer work, I was assigned to assist the bookstore with the book vendors, and I had some time before I had to pick up my grandson, so why not?! I love being at church; it is where I find my peace.

I walked to the table where I was assigned to serve, and I spoke to this nice-looking lady. "Hi," I said.

"Hi," She said. After that, CRICKETS! I was elated when my fellow men's ministry member, Daniel, came to the table. He was my friend and also the manager of the bookstore. His presence changed the atmosphere.

"Myles, have you met Kayla?" When I told Daniel that I had been standing there for fifteen minutes and she hadn't said anything to me, he said, "She does not like talking to people or them touching her."

"Yep, I learned that," I muttered.

She protested over Daniel's comment, and afterward, he assigned us some tasks to work on. Kayla and I had a very nice conversation for about three hours as we served the conference attendees. I thought she was cool, but I had to leave to pick up my grandson. I thought to myself, *Do I get the phone number? Nah, she works in the bookstore. I can find her.*

I said my farewell and left. As I walked down the hallway to exit the church, I thought for a moment about turning around. Then I remembered that my dad told me to never look back. So, I kept walking. I will see her in the bookstore on Sunday.

Heavenly Conversation # 3

The Trinity: Humm. Well, they haven't hardened their hearts. They just haven't fully opened their hearts. I love how they are both praying to Us. We will give them a little more time to heal, and then try it again. It will work out. We love them both so much because they have now turned their hearts to us regarding relationships. They just have to open their eyes and "see" their blessing. Aren't you glad We invented popcorn?

Myles

October – November 2019: The Gap

It's the first Sunday after the women's conference. Kayla said she served in the church's bookstore, so I figured I would drop by to say hello. I went to the bookstore around 11:00 after serving in the church's finance office. At the time, our church had services at 8 am, 10 am, and 12 noon. I could take several breaks between services since I was there for all the services.

As I walked around for a few moments, I spotted Daniel but not Kayla. I was not going to ask Daniel where she was because... well, I needed to be cool about this. I acted like I was looking for a book or something for around ten minutes. "I don't see her," I said to myself and headed back to the finance office. I thought of trying this again next week, but the second Sunday, the same thing happened—no Kayla. Third Sunday, no Kayla. Fourth Sunday, still no Kayla. Well, I guess it was not meant to be.

Kayla

October – November 2019: The Gap

I was emotionally and physically tired after the women's conference. I had served all day Friday and half a day on Saturday. The physical church could miss me for one Sunday. That

Sunday was spent lying around the house, watching the church service online, and having a pity party. This was long overdue, but it was a party of one—God never came to my pity parties.

I had a lot to be thankful for, but I was missing my mother, my father, and even my friends, who were only a phone call away. When a family member passes, people are around you immediately, but it's the weeks and months after that time that prove to be the most difficult. It is when you "remember" and second-guess yourself.

I know I truly did everything I could for my mother, and I know it in my mind, heart, and soul, but the end result was not something I could control. Life is up to God.

I served in the bookstore from 8:00 am to 10:30 am on the second and third Sundays in October. No signs of Myles, but it's okay—all in God's hands if it is meant to be. The fourth

Sunday in October, I headed to Norfolk for my college homecoming and to check on my mother's house. Dorothy was still there, but I still wanted to make sure everything was okay. While recovering from my pity party, my thoughts went back to the women's conference; of course, it was not the conference itself but rather Myles. Our church is very large, and I did not get his last name, but I was NOT going to ask Daniel, the bookstore manager (pride, lol). I rationalized it by saying that God was showing me that there are still good men in the world.

I will just keep praying; I am pretty sure my mother is interceding with God on my behalf.

To be honest, though, at this point in life, I did not believe something like love could happen to me.

I had been working for a Federal financial regulatory agency for over thirty-five years. Like most jobs, it had its ups and downs, but overall, it was a great company to work for, especially when considering the motivating factors: two 401ks, retirement, higher government pay, health benefits, paid federal holidays, and more. Even though I was eligible for early retirement, I had not set a date.

In preparation for it, and unlike other people, I prepared two people to replace me (yes, I am just that awesome). I worked with one lady for more than a year to take over a corporate project. She was beyond a blessing when my mother was sick and after she passed. Another gentleman was stepping up to lead a technical project I managed. He was a little reluctant to take the responsibility, but again, he also stepped up to the plate during my mother's transition.

People should always train and prepare others for their positions; I knew I would not be in that position for life. If you believe in Jesus Christ as Lord, you know what's for you is for you—at least that is how I have always thought. Plus, I never liked being told I could not go on vacation because there was no one to cover for me—ugh!

I traveled for my agency. My friends have always appreciated that aspect of my career. Why?

Because they like to "hitchhike" on my trips. "Kayla, make sure you get double beds," they would say. In my mind, I thought, *Why? Were you invited? Are you working on this assignment too?* My verbal response was always, "Okay."

My favorite software company hosted their annual conference in Las Vegas in November. I've attended this conference for the past five years all over the country. Over the years, I've gotten to know several of the participants and the company management team. In 2019, they asked me to serve as a moderator for a session on "Women in Technology." I was more than happy to do so, and with my company's permission, I led the session.

My friends Teresa and Brenda later called me on a conference call.

"Kayla, we heard you have to go to Las Vegas for work," said Teresa. "This is your first trip since your mother passed, and we decided you should not be alone in Las Vegas. We are coming to keep you company."

"There will be over 15,000 people at the conference. Some of my coworkers will be there. Also, not only am I attending, but I also have to serve as a moderator for a panel discussion. Are y'all coming to the conference? It is only $1,200." In my mind, I wanted to say, *Really? Hitchhikers!*

"Girl, we are not paying money to go to the conference! We are going to be there when you return to that empty hotel room. Make sure you get double beds," Brenda responded, laughing.

I said, "Okay," as usual. I flew to Las Vegas in the morning on the second Sunday in November, and they arrived later that afternoon. We had dinner and called it an early night because I needed to be up and ready for the conference by 8 am.

I got up at 6 am Monday morning to catch an Uber to the conference.

Brenda yawned and asked, "Kayla, can you please turn the lights down; we are trying to sleep."

Kayla, the word "NO" is good, and you should try it sometimes, I thought as I continued to get ready, ignoring her request.

"Ladies, y'all have a great day in the empty room," I said as I headed out. Mumbles of goodbye filled the room.

I went to the conference Monday through Thursday, and Teresa and Brenda went out to explore the Grand Canyon, Hoover Dam, and the Las Vegas strip. They were gracious enough to send me pictures during the day while I was WORKING! I got back late to the hotel, and for the most part, the conference provided dinner for me, or I would meet up with other associates at the conference.

There was a long line to get into the Thursday panel discussion and there was space for standing room only in the auditorium. I was pretty sure the crowd was only partially there for me but mainly for the Vice President of Information Technology or a major West Coast-based coffee company. The panel discussion went very well and given all that had already occurred earlier in the year, I had a good feeling about what happened. Also, the numbness of losing my mother this past summer was gradually lifting.

I offered to have dinner with the "hitchhikers" that Thursday after my successful moderation of the panel discussion. They were exhausted from a full day of excursions and decided to catch an early flight on Friday morning, but I still had another session to attend at the conference.

"That was fun hanging out with y'all," I said as they departed the hotel room—NOT.

It was all good, though; they were able to get away and enjoy themselves, which is what life is all about.

My Friday flight from Las Vegas to BWI was scheduled to leave at 12 pm. However, it was delayed, and I was feeling congested. I was in close proximity to around 15,000 people from all over the world, and as usual, my hotel room air was extremely dry. I had forgotten my sinus medication and traveling humidifier. This was going to be a long flight home. After a four-hour delay, we boarded the plane, just as I received a text from my friends letting me know they arrived home safely after deserting me for a 7 am flight. The flight was awful, and I felt beyond terrible when I landed that Friday evening. All the signs were there. I had a sinus infection and possible bronchitis (based on my WebMD degree).

Over the weekend, I was down for the count. Disappointment set in because I had not been to church since the third Sunday in October, and this was the third Sunday in November. I loved attending service in person, but online would have to work today, because there was no way I was going to church, let alone work on Monday. On Tuesday, I went to my doctor, who had a real medical degree, for a second opinion. The findings were as expected: sinus infection and bronchitis.

My manager suggested that I work from home for the rest of the week because she had "heard" some news about a new disease spreading in China. She was a nice person but had a major case of germaphobia. She said that given I had been around "foreigners," it would be best if I did not come into the office for the remainder of the week. Great! Another week for me to be around "lethargic Kayla" (better known as me), who was bordering on depression given the loneliness and the loss of my mother. She LOVED the holidays, especially Thanksgiving, which began in less than a week, and Christmas, which was a month away. Ugh, this season is going to be challenging.

Too bad my friends did not see it, but I had learned that unless you tell people what is really going on with you emotionally, they tend not to ask. If you share how you feel emotionally, it can be a downer, or they may feel obligated to do something about it. I completely understand because I do the same thing. I was so sick of my thoughts and memories. I just needed to get away because running away had always been my solution.

Chapter Five

Some One, From God

Some One, From God
I Need Love.
From someone who wants love,
From someone who gives love,
From someone who wants to receive love,
From someone who has love.
I Need Love.
From someone who knows love,
From someone who has been loved.
From someone who has lost love.
From someone who can make love.
For the Love I offer
Is real love,
Is complete love, and
Is provided through God's love.
I need love from someone…
Someone from God.
Spirit Inspired™ Someone From God© by Kay Henley

Myles

November 2019: Follow-up

I had not run into Kayla at church and had stopped looking for her. I believed that if God wanted me to connect with her, He would make it happen. Plus, it was now November, marking another first. After exercising and drinking some coffee, I was thinking about what I was going to do today when the phone rang.

"Dad," Mikael said, "today is Mom's birthday. Toni and I want to know what you want to do?" "Well, Son, what would you both like to do? Want to go to the cemetery and put flowers on her grave site?"

"Yes, Dad. Let's do that. We'll pick you up at noon," responded Mikael.

I knew what day it was—November 12. How could I not? I had known this woman for over 50 years, since she was 13. We had celebrated her birthday before the children were born, while they were growing up, and after they had families of their own. I knew what day it was and shed a few tears for the part of my heart that was now in heaven. Going to the cemetery was for the children. I knew she wasn't there, and I knew she would always be in my heart. They needed this. We laid flowers on her grave, shared our favorite stories, prayed, and then had a meal to celebrate her life as an excellent mother, a great wife, and most importantly, a child of God.

I came home after lunch, chilled, watched TV, and reflected on my past life and my current life. Just before I went to bed, I had one prayer request: I asked God to see Kayla again.

Kayla

Last Sunday in November 2019: You Have No One

I recovered from my illness and attended church service on the last Sunday of November 2019 after over a month. I attended the 8 am service and afterward served at the church bookstore. While I was assisting church members in finding various books, a retired coworker from my corporate employer came into the bookstore. We had known each other for over ten years, and he knew my mother had been sick.

Roland said, "Hi, Kayla! How is it going? How is your mother?"

Ouch! Hold it together. God, please do not let me cry when I respond. "Hi, Roland, my mother passed in June. I am hanging in here."

Roland responded, "Ahh, Kayla. That is so sad to hear. You have no mother, no father, no sister, no brother, no husband, no kids. Ahh, that is so sad."

I thought, *What the french fries? Even I don't curse in my head in church. But God, can I please take him outside and smack the "dog-poop" out of him?* After a deep breath, what came out was FROM GOD: "Well. I haven't given up on the husband."

That reality burned but in a non-harmful way. Roland was just being honest and real. We continued pleasantries until he left. He mentioned he served on the finance committee and was late going to count money after the first service of the day. He rushed off but promised to keep in contact.

I thought about what he said the rest of the day. He was right. I do not have any immediate family members. It's only me. After serving in the bookstore that day, I decided that I was not going to go home for the pity party. Instead, I went shopping! The retail therapy session that day was so beneficial. Thank God for the money to make it happen.

Myles

November 2019: The Call for the Setup

I had not been back to the church's bookstore since October. I decided that if God wanted us to meet again, He would have to make it happen. It was the fourth Sunday in November, and I was going through my regular routine: service, then as Chairman of the finance committee, overseeing committee members counting donations from the 8 am service.

"Where is Roland? He is late as usual," I said.

Roland walked into the room where two other committee members were waiting to count donations being delivered to the safe room.

"Roland, what took you so long to get down here?"

"I was in the church's bookstore, talking with someone I used to work with before I retired.

She lost her mother this summer and we were talking about how she was doing," Roland said. I asked, "What is her name?"

"Kayla."

"Kayla? I have been looking for her. I met her at the women's conference in October."

"Cool. Well, let's count the donations because I need to go home. My wife is waiting for me, and we need to do some things before the communion service this evening. We both have to be back here by 5 pm, and you still have to wait for the 11 am service donations."

We proceeded to count the donations, but I planned to follow up with Roland that evening, and I would check the bookstore again next Sunday. This was motivation. I wanted to see her.

Roland and Wendy

November 2019: Sunday Afternoon Conversation

Roland had the following conversation with his wife, Wendy on Sunday afternoon:

"Wendy, remember Kayla? We both used to work together at the same corporation before I retired.

"Yes, I remember her."

"Well, I dropped by the church bookstore after the 8 am service, and she told me her mother passed this summer."

"Ahh, that is so sad. We must keep her in our prayers."

"She has no immediate family but is still praying for a husband. This brings me to something else! Guess who met her last month and seems to be interested in her?" "Who?"

"Myles. Think we should set them up?" "Ahh, they would be a good fit. Let's do it!"

Myles

November 29: Conversation between Myles and Roland

"Myles, listen, are you really interested in meeting Kayla?" asked Roland.

"Yeah, man! I was going to mention that to you."

"So, Wendy and I are going to formally introduce you two."

Myles reminded Roland, "But I already met her."

In his excitement to orchestrate the connection, Roland said, "Man, let me do this. I am going to find her number, and we are all going to go out together next Saturday after Thanksgiving. I will call you once I talk with her."

Myles conceded to the eager Roland, saying, "Okay, sounds good. Thanks!

Heavenly Conversation #4

Peter: "See, it is coming together. I used a little human intervention, but We seem to be heading in the right direction."

The Trinity: "Yes, Peter, but expect a few bumps from her. She guards her heart because she trusts us with her professional career, travel, and family life, but not her love life. Strange, because we created love. We will ask her about that one day. This is new for her, but We know she will succeed. Now, about Roland's "communication" and what he said to her.

Peter: "Well, Roland's heart is in the right place. I am working with him on compassion and tact."

Kayla

November 2019: Thanksgiving Day

Before Thanksgiving, I told my family I was NOT spending Christmas with them. My mother LOVED Christmas. If there was anything to decorate in the house, it was decorated. The outside of the house, the mirrors inside, and even the refrigerator, washer, and dryer were decorated. Don't forget Black Santa Clauses all over the house. One year, one of the Black Santas moved, and my three-year-old cousin knocked it out! You go, kid!

I picked up one of my younger cousins from Richmond on the Tuesday before Thanksgiving and headed to Atlanta for the 2019 family Thanksgiving. The drive down to Atlanta was nice, and I had a great conversation with my young cousin, catching up on his life in Richmond.

Thanksgiving was at my cousin's house with her husband and two beautiful daughters, my uncle, his girlfriend, his younger son, and some of her in-laws.

That Thursday, Thanksgiving morning, I received a text on my cell phone with a 301 Maryland area code at 10:30 am. The text read, "Kayla, is this your cell phone number?" No name, but they obviously knew my name. Not cool. Plus, I am hundreds of miles away from Maryland. Also, why would anyone do robocalls on Thanksgiving Day? This must be a joke!

I texted back, "I don't know who this is, but if you don't respond in 10 minutes, I will be blocking your number!" No response, so I blocked the number.

The rest of the day was spent eating, fellowshipping with my cousins and extended family, and planning our shopping spree for "Black Friday."

Myles

November 2019: Thanksgiving Day

My son invited the family to his house for Thanksgiving. This would be my first Thanksgiving without my wife of 45 years. It was going to be different, but at least I would be surrounded by family. I would get through it.

(Phone rings)

Roland spoke proudly, "Hey man. Happy Thanksgiving. As you know, my wife and I decided to hook you and Kayla up.

I was excited to hear his news. "That sounds great, man."

But Roland had an unusual request. "Look. I need you to call her. She blocked my number."

I was confused and hesitated to make the call. "WHAT? I am not comfortable just calling her out of the blue. She may think I am some kind of pervert. Why did she block your number?"

"I don't know. I texted her and could not respond right away, so she blocked the number," said Roland.

I shook my head and chuckled. "Okay, I will call her, but it's going to take a minute. I am at my son's house playing with my grandkids and I need a minute to get my nerves up. I haven't done this in decades."

Kayla

November 2019: Thanksgiving Evening

The phone rang around 7:30 pm. I did not recognize the number just like I did not recognize the text number earlier that morning.

All of a sudden, I received a heavenly nudge from the Holy Spirit, telling me, "Answer the phone. Remember, you are in Atlanta; it could be about your house."

Okay, I will answer the phone, I said to my spirit in the midst of playing cards with my cousins.

"Hi, may I speak to Kayla?" said the voice on the other end of the phone.

Who else would answer my cell phone? "Hi, this is Kayla. Who is speaking?"

With a strong, confident voice, the response was, "Hi, this is Myles. I met you at the women's conference on the first Friday in October."

With a smile on my face, I walked away from the card game, seeking some privacy, to my cousins' shock.

"Oh yes. How are you today? Happy Thanksgiving."

"I am doing well. I am spending Thanksgiving with my son, his family, and extended family. What about you?"

"I am in Atlanta with my family. We just finished eating and mapped out our plans to go shopping tomorrow while playing cards."

"That sounds like family fun. I looked for you several Sundays after I met you. You said you served in the bookstore, but I didn't see you. I got there around 11 am for several Sundays," replied Myles.

Loving the fact that he was "seeking me," I responded, "I serve on the morning shift. I am usually gone by 11 am. I wish I had known." After several minutes of conversation, I couldn't help but wonder how he got my number.

As if Myles could read my mind, he said, "Well, I got your number from Roland, and he wants you to unblock him."

God! Wow. I must watch what I think. "I am definitely going to have to call Roland back," I said, laughing. "Myles, can I keep your number and call you sometimes?" I added in a flirtatious tone.

"I hope you do," he said.

Ahh suki, suki now. "It was nice talking with you, Myles," I replied.

"Nice talking with you too, Kayla."

I immediately hung up the phone and dialed Roland.

"Hi, Roland. Happy Thanksgiving."

"Kayla! What's up? Happy Thanksgiving. Why did you block my number?" Roland asked. "Roland, single woman here. Number one, – I did not have your number. Number 2, and most importantly, it is not appropriate to send a woman a text that states, "Kayla, is this your number?" without identifying yourself! Why didn't you call me back?"

"I was at Thanksgiving service at church. You know I sit on the front row," Roland responded.

I sighed and said, "Roland, and number three, you do not text while sitting on the front row in church!" I paused, shaking my head. "So, what's up?"

"Wendy and I want you to meet someone. When will you be back?" Roland replied.

"I am driving back from Atlanta on the Saturday after Thanksgiving."

"Well, leave early, so you can get here by 6 pm so we can all go out to dinner," he said.

"Roland, I did say I was driving back from Atlanta to DC on the Saturday after Thanksgiving, one of the worst days to drive, right? Also, I have to stop in Richmond and drop off my cousin. But who is it that you want me to meet? Is it Myles?"

"Don't worry about that right now. Just hurry up and come back."

"I will see what I can do, but I am not getting a speeding ticket."

That Friday, my cousins and I spent the day shopping. I thought about the conversation with Roland, but mostly, I thought about Myles.

The Saturday drive back to the DMV was extremely long and uneventful. We left at 7 am, and as expected, it took me 10 hours just to get back to Richmond.

At 5 pm, Roland called my cell phone. "Where are you?"

"I am just leaving Richmond. Can we do something tomorrow? It's been a long day and a long drive."

Roland said, "Man, I wanted to do it today. You are only three hours away."

"Me too, but traffic is bad. Let's do it tomorrow."

"Let me talk with everyone and get back with you."

"Okay." *Dude, I am tired, need a shower, and did I say I was tired?* Roland called back moments later. "Okay, let's get something after church service. Drive safely."

"Okay."

I arrived back at my townhome around 9:30 pm. Never again will I do that drive on a Thanksgiving weekend Saturday. I took a soaking bath for an hour, thought about Myles, and then went to bed. I was looking forward to Sunday, December 1, and I was praying that Roland wanted to introduce me to Myles.

December 1, 2019: It's Him

Sunday morning came, and I headed to church. I had someone more important to focus on: God. My day consisted of going to church service and then serving in the bookstore. We had a special guest artist that day, and Daniel asked me to assist the artist in the narthex. After listening to a powerful message, I headed to the bookstore. Daniel and I were setting up in the narthex when a FINE Black man and Roland walked toward me as only a Black man can!

Look at that WALK! Hal-le-lu-jah (as spoken by Tyler Perry's Madea). Daniel was looking at both of them in his now big brother mode like: "What are these two up to?" While Roland distracted Daniel, Myles came directly to me and said, "Hello, I am Myles

Robinson." My heart melted. I reintroduced myself and we shared pleasantries. After a few moments, Myles said, "I am on the church finance committee, and I have to return to the room with Roland to finish counting the offering." (I later learned he was the Chairman of the finance committee and had been for several years. Humble Myles was "someone" at the church). "Would you like to go to dinner with me in between services with Roland and his wife?" (Our church had four Sunday services at the time—8, 10, 12, and 6:30 pm—so there was no reason anyone who wanted a Word could not receive a Word on a Sunday).

"Yes, that would be nice," I responded.

"Okay, I will call you after we finish the noon service," Myles said with a beautiful smile. Myles and Roland strolled down the long hallway (cue the music in my head, "Cool in You" by Babyface). Daniel just looked at me and smirked.

Late Brunch

Roland and his wife called me at noon.

"Hi, Kayla, this is Roland. See, I told you who this is?" he said, laughing. We are looking forward to having dinner with you and Myles. Is it okay if Myles picks you up from your home?"

You introduced me to Myles, and NOW you are asking this question? Don't you know if your boy is safe? But I knew he was just asking from a "Christian proper" perspective. "All good," I said coyly. "I live in a gated community with nosy neighbors, and the house has cameras. If I don't want you in, you can't get in—without being noticed. Thanks for asking."

Myles arrived at 2:30 pm for our 3 pm dinner "date" with Roland and Wendy. After being let in the gate, Myles was standing at my front door. He rang the doorbell, and I peeked through the peephole. He had his back to the door, surveying the neighborhood, but I knew exactly who he was.

WOW! THIS MAN IS FINE! TRIPLE HOCKEY STICKS! I snapped out of my thoughts, trying to stop cursing in my head. I opened the door and greeted Myles.

"Hi, Kayla, are you ready to go?" he responded.

Cool, he did not ask to come in.

"Yes, let me lock up, and I will meet you outside the garage door."

BIG BONUS POINT #1 AND IT WILL CONTINUE THROUGHOUT OUR RELATIONSHIP:

He opened the car door for me (I am IN LIKE!).

We chatted on the drive to the restaurant. He asked about my Thanksgiving and my family. I responded and asked the same questions. The "new date" nervousness was in full force!

When we arrived at the restaurant, Roland and Wendy were already seated. The conversation was great until we got to one question.

Roland asked, "Are you going to the evening service with us?"

I found out that the three of them had to serve at the 6:30 evening service. I had already attended the 8 am service and served in the bookstore until 11:30. In my mind, my answer would be a "no," but the spirit within always has a different response.

"I had not planned to go," I said, looking into his eyes. "But I have no plans, so I can hang out with you all."

After the evening service (and a small wait for Myles, Roland, and Wendy to serve), Myles drove me home. He opened my car door and walked me the short distance to my front door. Myles shook my hand and said goodnight. I asked him to call me when he got home, and he did. I learned that he lived only 10 minutes from my house. Nice. We talked for a while on the phone that night, but we were both tired, so we said goodnight. It was a very good day.

Myles

December 2, 2019: First Dinner

Roland had done it! He set up dinner with him, his wife, and Kayla. I was excited because I had learned from my men's bible class that a solid Christian relationship should be started with an outing with another Christian couple. That Sunday, we had agreed to go out to have dinner at our local Silver Diner right after the finance committee had finished its morning duties.

"Wow," I muttered to myself as I drove into Kayla's community. "Not only is she only 10 minutes from my house, but she lives in a gated community! Cool."

I picked Kayla up from her townhouse and turned my back to the front door after ringing the doorbell. I did not want her to see how excited I was about this date.

"Hi, Kayla, are you ready to go?" I asked.

She was ready but needed to lock up first and would meet me outside her garage door." I didn't ask to come in; I did not want to be forward (old-school training), and we had to go to dinner.

She looked so beautiful as she emerged from the garage. *God is good,* I thought to myself. I opened the car door for her, and we were on our way.

We met up with Roland and Wendy at the Silver Diner. We had a great meal and engaging conversations, and after Roland asked, she even agreed to go to the evening service with us. I could tell Kayla was special, and I knew I would enjoy getting to know her.

Chapter Six

You Please Me

You Please Me
You please me by being my friend,
You please me with the time you spend.
You please me by telling me about our Savior,
You please me with your gestures and good-hearted nature.
You please me by being there when no one else is.
And never allowing me to forget who our Heavenly Father is.
For you please me with the things you do.
You please me...
By just being you.
Spirit Inspired™ You Please Me© by Kay Henley

Kayla

December 2, 2019: First "ONLY US" Date

Our first "official" date was the next day. I had tickets to see Anita Baker in concert with Wynter one of my sorority sisters, but when I got home that Sunday night, I called her and asked, "Wynter, would you mind if I took Myles to the Anita Baker concert tomorrow night instead of you?"

Without hesitation, Wynter responded, "Girl, I am so happy for you! Yes, do you, and call me when you get home... I need details!"

With that acceptance, I asked Myles out for our first date. He stated he would pick me up from my house to attend the concert. Promptly at 6 pm, Myles was at my door for the 7 pm concert.

"Thank you for going to the concert with me," I said.

Myles responded in a very humble voice, "My pleasure. I have not been to a concert in years." I knew his wife passed in 2019, but I had not asked about the details. I was glad that he could share this moment and time with me. For a 69-year-old gentleman, Myles looked GOOOOD. I learned he had a workout routine: Mondays, Wednesdays, and Fridays, he did resistance cycles and weights; Tuesdays and Thursdays, he did calisthenics. All I can say is that it worked VERY well for him (Praise the Lord!)

Anita Baker gave an awesome Christmas concert and even brought Lalah Hathaway to sing her father's song "This Christmas." At some point, I glanced at my date, and he was crying. "Myles, what's wrong?"

"I have so many emotions at this moment. Thank you so much. I will never forget this."

Wow, I scored brownie points on this one! I saw a beautiful heart in that moment, and it only grew during our relationship. How many men would be this humble and real on the first REAL date? God, please let this continue to be a beautiful experience. After the concert, Myles drove me home. In the car ride, he reached for my hand and held it until we arrived at my house. He walked me to the door, shook my hand, and said good night. He called me when he got home, and we talked for a few minutes. Before he hung up, he shared with me that before he closed his eyes to sleep, since he met me, he would say a prayer and goodnight to his deceased wife and then goodnight to me. My heart began to melt.

Myles

December 2, 2019: The Concert

Kayla and I had a wonderful dinner with Roland and his wife on Sunday. I couldn't believe I was engaging in a relationship with such a wonderful lady. Toward the end of our first dinner with Roland and Wendy, I caught a glimpse of Kayla talking to Wendy off to the side. The next thing I knew, Kayla asked me if I wanted to go with her to see Anita Baker in concert at the MGM on Monday, the next day. I was blown away! I was bowled over to know that someone wanted to do something for me as opposed to me doing something for them. Also, I had never seen Anita Baker in concert, but I listened to her albums. And I had never been to the MGM National Harbor in Maryland, even though it was only a few miles away. I had been fully dedicated to my late wife's inability to walk long distances and her illnesses, so it was something that I had never considered doing because I did not want to make her uncomfortable. Finally, a very attractive woman, whom I had a wonderful time with at dinner, asked me if I wanted to go out with her the following evening.

Not to seem too eager and to remain cool, I calmly replied, "Sure, Kayla. I do not have any plans for tomorrow evening. I can pick you up at 6 pm. My next thought was—*a date! WOW! To a concert that I didn't arrange! What should I wear to impress this wonderful angel?*

I went shopping Monday morning for the first time in years. I settled on a white form-fitting turtleneck to match up with a sports jacket I already owned. MGM National was decorated beautifully for Christmas. While we walked from the car to the hotel, I reached out and held her hand, something I had not done for quite a while, but something was tugging at my heart that guided me. We took a few pictures individually and together with the breathtaking decorations in the background. The concert started, and the tears started to flow. It was like I was in a dream—a well-known artist at a famous luxurious hotel and holding hands with a stunning woman. I tried not to let Kayla see that I was so emotional, but I didn't do such a good job of hiding it. It was like my heart was jumping out of my chest. I wanted to always keep this relationship between just the two of us.

When the concert was over, I didn't reach out to hold her hand. Instead, I grabbed her hand and wouldn't let go until I had safely seated her in the car. End of our first date.

Kayla

December 2019: Look at God!

After about a week, I shared with my prayer partner Sonia that I had met someone.

"Sonia, I met someone. He goes to our church. He is a really nice man."
"Ahh. That is nice. What is his name?"

"His name is Myles. Daniel from the bookstore initially introduced us on the first Friday in October during the women's conference. Myles came to support the event. We did not see each other anymore but God reconnected us after my friend Roland and I had a conversation and he hooked me up."

My prayer partner responded the way she always does by saying, "Let's pray that it works out."

Sonia and I proceed to pray about our daily blessings from God and share our requests and petitions.

A few hours later that morning, Sonia called back.

"Hi, Kayla. I was thinking. What is Myles's last name?"

"Robinson."

"Oh My God, Kayla! In January, we prayed for my cousin who happens to be Myles Robinson's wife. I introduced you to him at the movie in September."

"WHAT? Sonia, are you kidding me? Really? Wow. Look at God!"

So, Myles was her cousin who came into the movie theater late that September. So, God was trying to set us up then. It was at that moment I knew that God set this connection up, and I was NOT about to screw it up! I immediately called Myles and shared with him the details of my conversation with Sonia. He also understood at that moment that this connection, fellowship, relationship, whatever God wants it to be, was definitely set up by God. We both felt a little more connected at that moment.

Heavenly Conversation #5

Peter: Finally! I did it! Oh, sorry, You did it!

The Trinity: Well, it is not quite done yet, for her mother prayed for her to get married. You are halfway there. They both have to overcome some fears (false, evidence, appearing, real), but, Peter, you are correct; they now know Who connected them.

Kayla

December 2019: Getting to Know You Before Christmas

Knowing *WHO* connected us *(God)*, I felt a greater responsibility toward this man's heart and our relationship.

Over the next few weeks, we talked more about each other, discussing our hurts, pains, joys, friends, family, likes, dislikes, and so on. He shared a book his wife had written about herself and their relationship. I cried through several sections of the very honest book because it gave me an insight into her, their family, and the heart of my new friend.

Over the next few weeks prior to Christmas, Myles and I spent hours either on the phone or on dinner dates. While I was still working my "good quasi-government job," Myles was retired. I learned about his family (two children and three grandchildren), his siblings (two brothers), and most importantly, his deceased wife of 44 years and 51 weeks (she passed three days before their 45th anniversary). Courting was nice.

It was the first Christmas without my mother, though. I had told my family that I was NOT going to spend Christmas with them. I had decided I was going to Miami, lay on the beach, and wait for Christmas to pass. See, my mother LOVED Christmas! Not only because she MORE than recognized that Jesus was born to save her but also because of all the commercial aspects of the season.

EVERYTHING in her house had something that reflected the season. You experienced Christmas from the front of the house with all the lights on the outside. Then, once you walked in, EVERYTHING had something reflecting Christmas, from pillows on the sofa to bows on the lamps to her collection of multiple "Black Santas." There was not a room in the house, including the bathroom, kitchen, and laundry room, that did not have something that reflected Christmas.

Although the family was not gathering at my mother's house, I had decided that I did not want to be anywhere around anything that reflected the commercial aspect of Christmas.

But God.

God spoke to me that "avoidance" was not His plan for me this Christmas (ugh). He reminded me that *"I will not leave you comfortless; I will come to you."* (John 14:18) and that He would be with me (Isaiah 41:10), at my home during this season and always.

The Christmas Tree

Myles and I had made plans to have dinner on an early December evening after I finished work. As he glanced around my home, he asked, "Where is your Christmas decoration?" Myles asked. "Where is your tree?"

"I am not putting up any decorations! I have in the past, but I cannot do that this Christmas. My mother LOVED Christmas, so I am going to pass."

"Well, you at least need a tree," Myles responded.

This was our first argument. I hope he knew that (change the subject): "Well, thanks for the suggestion. Where are we going for dinner?"

As I was leaving church a week later, two weeks before Christmas, God spoke to me:

"Kayla, there is nothing wrong with having a Christmas tree. Go get one." *Really, I needed to hear that again. Again, just as plain as day.* As soon as the words came out of my mouth, I heard God specifically say, "Go to Lowe's. Get a Christmas tree."

So, I got my attitude together, went to Lowe's, and bought a Charlie Brown Christmas tree (God did not say how large). It was 3 feet tall. I set the box down in the hallway when I got home and called Myles.

"Hi, Myles, I bought a tree."

An excited Myles responded, "Awesome, I will come by and help you put it up."

I was looking forward to seeing him. Putting it up should not take long since it already had lights on it, so the only thing he needed to do was take it out of the box.

Myles arrived at my house about 5 pm that Sunday. I showed him the tree (still in the box). He pulled it out and stated, "It needs more lights."

In protest, I replied, "Myles, if it gets more lights, that tree will fall over!"

"I have an extra 5 feet of lights at home. I will go get them. I am sure this is not your first tree, so could you please grab your ornaments so we can put them on the tree?"

He said all of that with his usual beautiful smile, not knowing I was not smiling and pissed off inside. Not only was I not going to the beach but NOW there will be Christmas decorations in my house? Really? I was not feeling this at all. So, I decided to "call a friend" for a second opinion.

"Hi, Brenda. So, I met a guy, and I was really beginning to like him."

"Wow, that is awesome! Where did you meet him? What is his name?"

I was immediately irritated with her because she wanted details, and I just wanted validation regarding not putting up a tree. "Girl, please with the questions. I don't have time for that! You know I told y'all I was not doing Christmas this year. Not only did God tell me I could not go to the beach, but he also told me to buy a tree, and now this guy wants me to put it up and hang ornaments on it!"

Brenda, in her normal sarcastic way, replied, "The nerve! Kayla, just get the bulbs, you have them, and have them ready when he comes back. Your mother would have wanted you to decorate and have a tree up for Christmas. She would have wanted you to celebrate the birth of Christ. Remember that is what Christmas is about—it is not about you."

Did the phone drop, or did I just hang up? Either way, that was the end of that conversation. I did not see a Christmas tree in the Bible, but I understood the message from God, Brenda, and Myles: stop avoiding life. Then I remembered: Myles's wife passed away in January of this year (his first Christmas without his wife), and he was still celebrating Christmas. So, I went through my Christmas boxes and got out my favorite ornaments. About 20 of them (out of the 100 I had in storage).

Myles came back around 20 minutes later with 5 feet of multicolored lights. I was still in my "feelings," so I sat in my oversized, comfortable chair and watched him put the lights and ornaments on the tree.

Watching Myles set up the tree, I realized how handsome, nice, and kind this man is who God brought into my life. "God, I really want this to work." I sat there because this was becoming hard. It reminded me of a lot of emotions I had suppressed. This would be my first Christmas without my mother. It had only been me and her for decades. I mean I have family, but that was my mother. I started reminiscing how we spent last Christmas together last year; how much different this and all the years to come would be without her.

Myles was talking, but I did not know what he was saying until he said, "I am getting ready to go."

"You are leaving? Aren't you taking this tree with you?"

With a comforting smile, Myles said, "No, the tree stays here, and you will be blessed by it."

He shook my hand and left.

The house now had a heavy silence, but I did not feel alone. I returned to my comfortable oversized chair, which was in front of the 3-foot tree, which Myles had placed on a table. The tree was beyond beautiful and seemed to have an extra glow to it. Instead of being "fuddy-duddy" in my feeling, I sat there thinking. I was remembering the love of my parents while receiving love from my Heavenly Father.

I let the memories flow from my childhood with my parents to times with cousins during the holidays. I did not need pictures; it was all in my heart. The Holy Spirit was there with me, reminding me:

"'For I know the plans I have for you,' declares the Lord, 'plans to prosper you and not to harm you, plans to give you a hope and a future." Jeremiah 29:11

"For I consider that the sufferings of this present time are not worth comparing with the glory that is to be revealed to us." Romans 8:18

"And my God will meet all your needs according to the riches of his glory in Christ Jesus." Philippians 4:19

"Fear not, for I am with you; be not dismayed, for I am your God; I will strengthen you, I will help you, I will uphold you with my righteous right hand." Isaiah 41:10

"Surely, Lord, You bless the righteous; You surround them with Your favor as with a shield." Psalm 5:12

"He healeth the broken in heart, and bindeth up their wounds." Psalm 147:3

"The LORD will guide you always; he will satisfy your needs in a sun-scorched land and will strengthen your frame. You will be like a well-watered garden, like a spring whose waters never fail." Isaiah 58:11

"Casting all your care upon him; for He careth for you." I Peter 5:7

"For God hath not given us the spirit of fear; but of power, and of love, and of a sound mind." 2 Timothy 1:7

"And we know that all things work together for good to them that love God, to them who are called according to his purpose." Romans 8:28

I sat in that chair for the rest of the evening and half the morning, with God's peace steadily overtaking my fears and life concerns while giving me unbelievable peace and comfort. I know I had grieved my mother after she passed, but this was a true release. I thanked God for the parents He blessed me with, how they raised me, and the ability to begin looking forward to the future.

My heart opened more to God that night. I gave it all to Him via prayer, praise, and tears that seemed to have no end. I knew God just wanted me to speak my heart because putting up a strong façade was not who He knew I was inside. I needed to sit still and allow Him to heal me His way, and He did. See, that night I was reminded who held my future because I did not know what the future held at that time or where this "thing" with Myles was heading. I did know one thing that God confirmed that night: He had me through it all, and I surrendered it all to Him. That tree stayed up until the middle of January, and I was with it and my Heavenly Father every night, for hours, in my oversized chair.

My bestie, Teresa, had invited me to spend Christmas with her friend and her family. Wow, spending time in a family atmosphere, just what I did not want! I gave in to God and my friend and agreed to come. I was thinking I could tolerate anything for an hour.

Myles spent Christmas with his son, daughter-in-love, daughter, three grandkids, and in-laws. It was his first Christmas, and his children were without their mother. He had not told them about me, which was fine because he wanted to wait a full year for them to deal with their feelings.

Myles was fine because he was the best husband to his wife; he did all he could based on the Word of God, so everything else he left in God's hands. It was God's decision to call his wife home and Myles had made peace with it.

After we spent Christmas with others, we spent an hour on the phone chatting. We decided to wait until the next day to see each other. For me, I spent the rest of the evening thinking about past Christmases with my family. I am sure Myles did the same because this was "new" for both of us.

Myles

December 2019: First Christmas Without My Wife

"Grandpa, will you play with us?" was the request from my two grandchildren on Christmas Day. It was the first Christmas since my wife passed. My immediate and extended family had our traditional Christmas family breakfast, opened a few presents, and were now getting ready for the traditional Christmas dinner.

"Sure, guys, I will play with you all."

This Christmas felt different. I had to decorate the house and put up the tree by myself. No one was around to comment on the decorations or even complain about how I decorated. I was lonely this Christmas, but I was not alone. "Myles, you are going to get through this day," I said to myself. "Everything will be fine. Tomorrow will be here before you know it."

As I played with my grandchildren, I said, "My loves, are you sure this is how we are supposed to play this game or are you both pulling Grandpa's leg."

They giggled. *Yes. I am going to get through this day.* I went home that night and called Kayla to say goodnight. We both got through this first Christmas without our loved ones.

Kayla

January 2020: A New Year, A New Relationship

"Happy New Year!" I said to everyone around me. I was starting the New Year in church as in past years. I LOVED IT!

This year was different because I had a date AFTER welcoming the New Year at Church (watch out now!). Myles and I did not go anywhere. He picked me up for service, drove me back to my house, talked for a few minutes, and went home (hey, we are over 40, 50, 60, etc.). I had not been to his home yet, and in a way, I was cool with that. He and his wife had built that home from scratch, and she passed in the house. I had some "thoughts" about it, but it was too early in the relationship for those concerns. When I crossed that road, I decided I would give it to God.

During January, we hit the concert circuit. I was so happy that he loved concerts. This "dating" month was consumed with dinner, concerts, dinner, conversations, repeat, repeat, repeat. We saw Diana Ross and one of my favorite jazz artists, Keiko Matsui, at the Kennedy Center.

Myles became quiet during the middle of January. Then I remembered: it was almost one year since his wife passed.

"Myles, what do you and the children have planned for the first remembrance year of your wife's passing?"

"I had not thought about doing anything, Kayla. We probably will just go to the cemetery."

"Myles, can I suggest you host a remembrance ceremony for her? You invite all the family over and have everyone share their favorite memory of Valerie. I can help you plan it and create the

invitation and program."

"Kayla, you would do that for me?"

"Sure. Also, I think you should give your guest seeds from your wife's favorite flower or plant. The flower or plant seed would be a way for them to always remember her."

"Wow, thank you, Kayla."

Myles prepared all the food and hosted family and friends for the three-hour ceremony. Myles came over to my house after the ceremony and shared highlights of the event. He said everyone appreciated the fellowship, especially his children. I cannot imagine how he felt. After he got through talking, I held him in the silence of the room while he drifted off in reflection.

Myles

January 2020: Remembering

This was an awkward time in my life. January 16 was the day God saw fit to take my late wife to be with Him. I know she was with Him because she had always loved the Lord. The other difficult time for me was that January 19 would have been our 46th wedding anniversary. Our kids had made it through a whole year without their mother. The one-year anniversary of her passing was a huge elephant in the room.

After 45 years of being around relatives on her side of the family, they all became my family as well, not to mention they were truly relatives of our kids – cousins, uncles, aunts, etc.

This was one year without her. I knew everyone was looking at me to see what and how I would mark and handle this anniversary. When I was dating Ms. Mermaid, I told one of her uncles that I would wait at least one year before I married again out of respect for her and her family. Ms. Mermaid did not like that, which was one of our issues.

Now, I was very, very serious about Kayla. Kayla was the most supportive and understanding person I had ever met. She suggested a memorial ceremony with such details that was much, much more than I could have ever come up with. She designed a flyer for the family and came up with the idea of giving a packet of seeds to each person for them to plant in her memory. The kids and I visited the grave site to put flowers on it. Everything went well. My wife's family loved the ceremony. The positive feedback I received from the family was confirmation that Kayla was the perfect person for me.

This was something I couldn't have done on my own. Kayla was a woman of many talents. I found out that not only was she a tech-savvy financial expert in the banking regulatory industry and very easy on the eyes, but she was also a published poet. In my mind, we would be excellent together—physically, spiritually, and intellectually.

Chapter Seven

I Will Show You Love

I Will Show You Love
I will show you love,
The way God meant it to be.
Not about the physical body,
Not about what you naturally see.
I will show you a relationship,
Based upon God's Word.
Not about what you feel and believe,
Not based upon what you have heard.
I will show you the love I have,
That should be shared by two.
Not done by worldly rules,
But done, as God needs two to do.
God wants the best for us,
Sent by His love from above.
Through God, I will give you the best,
I will show you love.
Spirit Inspired™ I Will Show You Love© by Kay Henley

Myles

February 2020 – When You Know, You Know

"Will you marry me?" That was the question I asked Kayla on the first Saturday in February.

After two months of dinner dates, movies, concerts, long late-night conversations like I was a teenager again, and various fellowships with friends, I knew she was the one. God blessed me with her for this season of life. So, while we were out on one of our weekly excursions, I got up the nerve and asked her to be my wife. It was not that I was lonely or rebounding from a long marriage. I knew Kayla was the right partner for me, and I was ready to commit. It was a casual proposal (no ring yet), but Kayla's response was "yes," and that was all that I needed.

Kayla

February 2020: Is This Really Happening?

We went to a Virginia Winery on the first Saturday in February. I like wine but only the sweet ones (as my doctor commented, "elevated Kool-Aid"), and I love the beauty of a vineyard.

We checked out three Loudoun County, Virginia wineries, but what happened at one of them left me in shock.

Fabbioli Cellars is a beautiful octagon-shaped building with a tasting room on one level and a relaxing sitting area upstairs. The grounds are full of vineyards and also have outdoor seating, but this was February, and although it was a warm day, we stayed inside. We selected our wines, ordered a charcuterie board, walked upstairs, and began our fellowship conversation as usual. This time, though, he seemed a little nervous. So, he got to the point:

"I am in love with you. I do not need to date a long time to know when a person is right for me. I love our conversations, I love your beauty, and most importantly, I love how you love God. Kayla, will you marry me?" said Myles.

WHAT? Is this really happening? Don't choke on your food. Open your mouth and speak because you know the answer is going to be yes.

"Myles, I am in love with you too. Yes, I will marry you."

It was simple, it was beautiful, and it was him. I knew my mother was beaming, and then it hit me: I had just agreed to marry someone! Where is the ring? I have not met his children, grandchildren, or family. And where exactly does he live? I haven't been to his house yet. And do I really want to go? Where will we live? Questions poured into my head but the only ones that came out were:

"Where is my ring? Are you sure? Oh, that is right, we cannot officially get engaged until we take the church's premarital class," I replied in an excited and nervous tone. I heard that the Ministers for the class at church, "So You Think You Want to Get Married," suggested not buying the ring before you get engaged because your decision may change after the class. The ring may make you feel obligated if you make the full decision prior to the class. Great point!

In his calm, compassionate voice, Myles responded, "I will check to see when the next premarital class will be held and sign us up. Yes, I am sure, and I want you to know that I am committed to you from now on and as long as the Lord sees us together."

My eyes brimmed with tears. "I SO thank God for you, and I, too, am committed to this love journey with you." Wow, that was corny. I gave him our first soft kiss on the lips.

The cool thing about being with Myles is that I felt he was my best friend, and most importantly, I felt emotionally safe. I felt comfortable sharing my dreams, fears, and pain with him, and I knew he felt the same way. We talked about EVERYTHING, and there was no judgment. We both knew God was the ultimate Judge. We both walked into the relationship knowing we had a past and past relationships (again, we were over 40, 50, 60—you get it). We were just focused on getting to know and learn from each other. On the way home from the vineyard, we stopped by a jewelry store (he wanted to see what type of ring style I liked), but I had no clue. No one had asked me to marry them since I was in my 30s, and I had not thought about it since then. Nothing was purchased, but it was a joy just looking.

Heavenly Conversation #6

Peter: "Praise the Lord! My work here is done!"

The Trinity: "Peter, not yet. Her heart is saying yes, but her mind is still guarded. She is almost there, but she is not used to having a man treat her the way Myles has been treating her. She will come around, but she still has some growing and more trusting in Me to do. Also, Myles will have some upcoming obstacles with his family and friends. Remember, his wife passed a year ago. Peter, you need to hang around to see how this will end, although we already know."

Peter: "You know, you all really make this guardian angel thing challenging for me, but I am on it!"

Kayla

February 2020: Valentine's Day Appearance

Our church's couple ministry hosts a couple's fellowship every February. Unmarried couples in committed relationships are invited to attend the night of fellowship. It is an opportunity for married and committed couples to participate in a godly fellowship. It was the first time Myles and

I had made an official appearance at a church event. I did not know who Myles was in the church until this event, and people were watching me.

I did not know how well-loved he was among church members. So many people congratulated us on being a couple (they did not know we were engaged) and shared with me the character of this awesome man. They were telling me about his compassionate spirit, his patience with people, and his sharing heart.

A random church woman, whom I did not know, said to me, "Girl, you dating Myles? You got a good one. He is one good-looking man. There were so many women waiting for him to grieve after his wife died. Myles handled that grief very well. How did y'all meet?"

I responded without a "mind your own business" look, "Long story on how we met, and I agree, he handled his grief well."

That night, I fell so much more in love with this blessing God has placed in my life.

Myles

Valentine's Day 2020: Valentine's Day Appearance

Our church is large, but it is also small. Kayla mentioned she had been a member for over seven years, but given the fact that we had never met, I wasn't sure she fully comprehended how well-connected I was at the church.

Additionally, after my wife passed and I returned to church, the Honeys were on the prowl. I received dinner plates, cakes, invites to dinners, phone numbers of friends who had a sister, aunt, cousin, or even mother, who was looking for a good man. Church people saw me as a prize, and they all wanted to give this award to someone they knew. I was not ready for that, and I truly thank God for protecting me from it.

However, this was an opportunity for me to show church people that God made the selection for me, and they could back off. I also had friends at the dinner who were checking Kayla out, but I knew she was a blessing from God and confident it would all work out.

I stepped away from Kayla to talk with a male church friend, who said, "So that is her? She is beautiful! Did y'all meet at church? She got any friends? My son needs a good woman."

"Yes, she is," I replied as I observed Kayla from a distance. "You ask a lot of questions.

Also, let God bless your son in his time with a woman. Stop hunting for him," I said while walking away.

The evening confirmed what I knew, and we had a great time fellowshipping with everyone. After taking her home, I went back to my house and decided that it was time to move on from saying goodnight to my deceased wife.

Kayla

February 2020: Celebrating You

Myles's birthday was two weeks after he asked me to marry him. I wanted to make it special. Myles is a beautiful spirit who has been through a lot over the years, but he relied on God through it all. Now, this man wants to marry me? Thank you, Lord.

I introduced him to my world. Yes, I know, it is his birthday and not about me, but hey, I am going as well (smirk).

"Myles, I have an exciting day for you today," I said when I called him on his birthday. "Kayla, I don't want anything special."

"Remember, I am an only child. All birthdays are special," I exclaimed. Myles responded, "Okay, I am game."

We had dinner at a seafood restaurant in downtown Silver Spring, Maryland. The after-dinner activity caught Myles by surprise.

"Dinner was great," he said. "Thank you. This is nice and simple, just as I had hoped, although dinner was a little pricey. Delicious but a little pricey. Are you sure you don't want me to contribute to the cost?"

Wow! Did he really offer that?

"Ahh, thank you, but I got this. Now on to part two, a couple's massage."

Myles's face said it all—surprised. I looked into his eyes. He gathered his thoughts and had a more subdued smile. We would be in the same room, on separate tables, divided by a partition.

"Kayla, as you probably saw from my facial expression, I thought this was going to be something different," Myles said with a chuckle. "This was a pleasant surprise, very nice, and it was just what I needed."

Afterward, we went back to my place and talked for a while. It was an incredibly romantic day, something he claimed to have not experienced in a long time.

Myles

February 2020: Celebrating me

I had not done anything for my birthday in years. My wife had been sick for several years, and prior to that, no one really made a big deal about it—until this year. I have never felt so appreciated.

We had planned an intimate dinner at "All Set" in downtown Silver Spring, Maryland. Kayla ordered the salmon, and I had the surf and turf. Dinner was great, and then she capped it off with a couple's massage session.

Kayla told me she loved massages, and honestly, I could not wait to give her a personal massage. That would be in the future, but tonight I was looking forward to what she had planned. We went to a chain massage service near the restaurant.

The masseuse came into the room. Kayla had requested a woman for me and a man for her for the one-hour session. They provided us with the instructions and shared what they would be doing. We were in the same room, separated by a curtain, but it was still an intimate setting. We lay on our respective tables, and the next thing I knew, the hour-long massage was over. I did not know how much I needed that massage. We got dressed (behind the curtains), walked to the car, and drove home. I definitely was "All Set" and ready to marry Kayla.

Kayla

February 2020: No Passionate Kissing!

I know me. I love to kiss! I love those long, lingering, wet kisses for several minutes at a time. I get excited just thinking about it. Let me state now that I am no saint. Please, I have been single all my life. Just being real. Now, in the past three years, I have been celibate, but it was for multiple reasons:

- It's a sin (that I wanted to stop breaking)

- Busy at work

- Dating sucked

- My mother died

I felt when she wasn't fellowshipping with all her family and friends and worshipping.

God in Heaven, then she was looking at me (all about me—only child coming out). I decided I would not do the heavy kissing with Myles until after the wedding. But the cuddling got a little heated when he returned to my house after his birthday celebration. He may have been a little older, but the brother was *PHine* (meaning a doctorate in good-looking)!

When he leaned in for the kiss, I literally ran to the door. I knew nothing would have happened because of his character. He did not know my seductive powers, though—but I did! Plus, I had not had "relations" in over 36 months, 30 days, and 15 hours (but who was counting?).

I explained what I thought about kissing and how it affected me. He looked at me strangely but without judgment and stated he understood and respected my position. I gave him a long, compassionate hug, and he left. *YES! I am marrying THAT man! Awesome! Thank you, Jesus!*

Myles

February 2020: Her No Kissing Rule

Kayla stated that she did not want to kiss. I found that interesting and concerning. It made me wonder about how she wanted to connect emotionally while understanding her concerns at the same time. I wanted that affection right now, but I wanted her more for the long term. So, we compromised. We cuddled when watching movies, and we held hands as much as possible. I could truly wait for God's best for me because I have waited this long.

Kayla

February 2020: Going to His House

One Sunday in February, after service and after the marriage proposal, Myles invited me to his house. I had not been to his house since we started dating, although we only lived ten minutes from each other, and I had absolutely no problem with that. I had mixed emotions about going to his house. Myles and his wife had spent over thirty years in the home. Their children grew up there, and the grandchildren regularly visited. They had family functions there. She passed in the home. I was anxious, but then I remembered that the Lord knew all of this. God created this relationship (Philippians 4:6).

We entered through the two-car garage, and what did I see? My dream car. My friends know that I've always wanted a candy apple red Mercedes Sport Coupe Convertible, a two-seater with white

interior. What did Myles have in his garage? A dark red Mercedes Sport Coupe, 2-seater with beige interior (God knew that white would get dirty). Look at God, dotting the i's and crossing the t's. Talking about giving me the desires of my heart. *Won't He do it!*

"Nice car, Myles," I said, looking at the convertible. "Yes, it was my wife's car." She definitely had great taste, not only in a man but also in a car.

We had dinner and he continued to show me around the house. Nice house, with three levels: living room, dining room, library, kitchen, family room on the main, and upstairs, there were three bedrooms (one converted to an office), hall bathroom, master with a sitting room and his and hers walk-in closets. There was also a massive bathroom with a shower and tub.

The house was over 3,000 square feet, but my favorite room was the unfinished basement. I knew he wanted me to move into his home, and I initially had reservations until I saw the basement. I walked down those stairs, and a light bulb went off in my head, which was confirmed by Myles stating, "The basement is unfinished, but you can do whatever you want with it."

Is this man in my head or what?!? I kindly responded, playing it cool, "Oh, okay."

Nothing but open space and my creative juices were rolling, jumping ahead of everything, and thinking about how I could create this space. My only concern was the bedroom. Myles had shared that his wife passed in his arms in bed in the master bedroom.

At the end of the tour, I asked, "Myles, this is a beautiful home. One question, though—did you change the mattress?"

Myles responded compassionately and with a loving smile, "Yes, I did."

Still, my mind was racing, and I think he knew it. As we chilled in the family room watching TV, a peace came over me, and I heard God saying clearly, "Kayla, it is just a house." I did not have any issues going to the house after that. This was going to be my home.

Myles

February 2020: First Visit to My House

I did not ask Kayla to visit me at my home initially. Why? I believe a man should pick a woman up from her home for dates. We were not sitting around each other's homes. Instead, we were going out—movies, plays, concerts, dinner, and wineries. There could be no issues when we were outside the home.

I had concerns, though, when I invited her to my home. My wife passed in our bedroom; my

children spent their teenage years in the house, and there were so many memories over the past twenty-five years experienced and created in the house. Also, I was praying that once we were married, we could live in my house instead of purchasing a new home. The mortgage was paid off. I did not want to go back into debt.

I gave Kayla a tour of the house, but it appeared that the main area she was excited about was the basement.

"Wow, it is unfinished," exclaimed Kayla. "So many possibilities."

"You can design any way you like," I said.

I don't think she was expecting that answer. *Got her.*

Kayla

February 2020: What in the World?

I had not shared with my coworkers yet that I was getting married because Myles and I still had to attend premarital classes. It was late February 2020 and people were abuzz about a virus spreading throughout the world. My quasi-government job told us to be prepared to work from home (which I absolutely had no problem with accommodating their request). I did not believe that a virus would send every government worker home. I thought back to how sick I was in November after that International Technical Conference. I thought maybe it was God purging me in preparation for this relationship. Either way, I remembered how sick I was and truly thanked God for healing me and my manager for encouraging me not to come to work for that November week.

Myles

March 2020: Meeting the Children

Will my children react favorably with my choice for a wife? This was a nervous concern I asked myself. Why? Because of the issues that had occurred with a previous relationship with Mermaid. They also adored and loved their mother and knew we both loved each other and were committed for better or worse.

I believe they learned from our relationship that marriage has highs and lows, but through it all, God is in the center, the glue in a marriage, and that *love covers a multitude of sins by everyone* (1 Peter 4:8).

My first effort to entertain another woman after being married for forty-five years was quite awkward. After I met Kayla, it was different. It worked out well.

From December through January, we spent a lot of time together, either in person at dinners, concerts, plays, or on the phone. I felt like a teenager again. I was very impressed with her as she was with me.

I thought to myself, *Okay, now it's time to tell the kids, especially given I had asked her to marry me. How would they react to their only surviving parent marrying another woman?*

I called Mikael.

"Hi, Dad. Everything good? What's happening?"

"Mikael, I am doing great! I met someone and I would like you and your sister to meet her. Can you meet me at the Silver Diner on Thursday evening?" I asked.

"Sure, Dad," he replied.

I called Toni next.

"Hi, Dad. How you doing today?" She paused. "Everything good?"

"Yes, Toni, all is great. I met someone and I would like you and your brother to meet her. Can you meet me at the Silver Diner on Thursday evening?"

We settled on a quick dinner date in early March. It was a great dinner meeting, with everyone engaging in conversation and getting to know each other. I felt it went well. I remember my daughter wanted to make sure

Kayla did all she could to keep her dad safe during COVID-19, especially since she and her brother had children. At the time, COVID was affecting older people more than younger people.

My children gave me their blessing to continue with the engagement and seeing Kayla. I also knew all was okay with the kids because not only did they ask Kayla for her telephone number (probably to do a background check), but they also let me pick up the check, as usual.

Even during the most difficult time in the country, I was blessed to have an opportunity to date a woman of my choice and my kids accepted her. The whole world was shut down, limiting travel and group outings. Kayla and I had plenty of time to get to know each other during this time, which was just perfect with me.

Kayla

March 2020: Meeting His Children

Myles organized a dinner on the first Thursday in March for me to meet his son and daughter.

His oldest son has two children, a boy and a girl. His daughter has a son. I was nervous about meeting them because I knew they did not like the previous one and their mother had passed away a little over a year ago. I had no clue if they were still grieving because everyone grieves differently.

We all gathered at a local diner. As we ordered our meals, the "polite" interrogation began.

Mikael and Toni asked a series of questions, starting with, "Tell us about yourself. Where are you from? Where do you live? Where do you work? How did you meet our father?"

"I am from Norfolk, and I live about seven miles from your father. I work for a government agency, and I met your father through mutual friends at church," I replied confidently. "We were introduced three times before we really started talking. First by your cousin Sonia, a gentleman named Daniel at a conference, and finally, by a deacon at the church. Yes, I am a member of the church, but I did not meet your father until this year. Finally, my prayers are with your family for the anniversary homegoing of your mother."

After additional questions and discussions among all parties, the main question was asked.

"If y'all met less than six months ago, why are y'all getting married so soon? No reflection on you, Kayla, but my mother just died a little over a year ago. I am still mourning." Mikael said.

Myles stepped into the conversation and stated, "Look, I loved your mother. I had known her since I was sixteen and she was thirteen. We were married for almost forty-five years. She was my high school sweetheart and an excellent and loving wife and mother. I did my best to be the best husband and provider. We had a great marriage. I am not getting any younger, though, and I love the companionship of a woman. I prayed about it, and I know Kayla will be the perfect fit for me."

"Dad, I can respect that. Thank you, and Kayla, we look forward to getting to know you better," Mikael replied as Toni agreed.

Wow! That was not too bad. Over the course of the next few months, I learned more about their mother, the children, and the grandchildren. As mentioned, Myles's wife had even written a book about her life. It was one of THE most transparent and real books I have ever read. She had a beautiful spirit, and I learned to respect her even more after reading the book and conversing with Myles and their children. God had truly blessed me with a beautiful family.

Kayla

March 2020: The List

That meeting triggered my memory. I had written a list of what I wanted in a husband, inspired by the movie War Room. When I got home that night, I went to my prayer closet, where I had posted the list. I had not been in the prayer closet since my mother passed due to all the memories. But that night, I went in there and read the list of qualities I wanted in a man:

1. I wanted a man who loved God and is an active member of a Bible-believing church. *(Check! Myles is not only a member of my church but also head of the finance committee and is in the process of becoming a deacon in the church.)*

2. I wanted a man who was financially stable. *(Check! Myles is a retired financial institution executive, debt-free, and did I mention, head of the finance committee, an extremely important and trusted position for our church, which also means Myles had great character AND he owned his own home DEBT-FREE.)*

3. I wanted a man who had grown children with no drama, and grandchildren would be a plus. *(Check! Myles's children are very kind, and the grandchildren are adorable).*

4. I wanted a man who worked out and focused on being physically fit. *(Check! Myles works out M-W-F on a cycle, does weights, and T-T-H calisthenics. The brother is in excellent physical condition.)*

5. I wanted a man who was not intimidated by my career and confident in himself. *(Check! Myles had his own successful career in*

finances, and he walked with the confidence of God in his spirit.)

6. I wanted a man who would be patient with me and all my good and bad points. *(Check! We talk about everything. He listened, and if action was needed, he made it immediately. His ability to do that made me do the same for him.)*

7. I wanted a man who had a heart for others, giving of both their time and money. *(Check! Myles encouraged other young men in his church and outside of church. He kept his relationship with former coworkers, Black, White, or any race or social status while never compromising his faith.)*

God blessed me with the man who was right for me, and yet, I still struggled to believe this was happening because he was so right for me.

Kayla

March 2020: The Pandemic, Go Home

"*Go home.*" Those were the words out of my manager's mouth at a staff meeting on the second Wednesday in March. The government decided to shut down due to the pandemic. With just a two-day notice, we were told we had to work from home until further notice. I did not know at the time that it would be the last time I would be in my office.

Myles's children held a conference call with Myles and me and reminded us that because they had young children and did not know what this virus was and its impact, it would be okay if I checked in on their father. That was a done deal for me.

Over the next few months, while waiting to take the church's condensed virtual premarital class, we spent every weekend getting to know each other. We went walking and took rides to outside venues, all things that were Covid-doable.

March 2020: Monuments Visit

As Myles brought me home one March night evening, he matter-of-factly mentioned, "I have never been to the Veteran Memorial in DC. For that matter, I have never been to the Martin Luther King Memorial or the Roosevelt Memorial."

I thought, *Dude, you were born in DC! You have lived in this area for decades!*

This makes sense. Most people in their local communities rarely visit historical venues in their local community.

"Let's go now," I said.

"Okay." Myles appeared excited.

I think he agreed primarily because he was not ready for the night to end. Off we went to Washington DC, a twenty-minute drive from my house at 9 pm. The monuments are beyond beautiful at night, especially those around the pond. We first toured the Martin Luther King, Jr. Memorial and then walked to the Franklin Delano Roosevelt Memorial.

We then drove over to the Vietnam Veterans Memorial and perused all the names on the wall. Finally, we walked up the stairs to the Lincoln Memorial and sat on the steps for a moment, admiring the Washington Monument as it appeared in the reflection pond.

We spent around two hours at the monuments, and I fell even deeper in love watching this man tear up at the wall as he remembered his time in the military while enjoying the beauty of the city and our relationship. He did get a kiss (nothing fancy) on

the steps of the Lincoln Memorial to celebrate the beauty of it all. It was a spontaneous, simple, beautiful way to end our date night.

Myles

March 2020: Monument Visits

I was born in Washington, DC and grew up in Prince George's County, Maryland. I had been to the Washington Monument while in high school, but I had never, in my over sixty years on earth in the area, visited the Lincoln, Jefferson, Martin Luther King, Jr., Roosevelt, or Vietnam memorials. I had not explored my hometown in decades, mainly because seeing the memorials required a lot of walking. I didn't have any problem walking around, but my late

wife's problems with her knees, and later both being replaced, made it nearly impossible for her to do any extended walking. Kayla, in her spontaneous way, decided this was the moment that would change. I was overwhelmed by her desire to do things out of her heart that were dear to me without asking.

In a moment of spontaneity, we got in the car and drove downtown to visit the monuments. We spent time at each monument reading the inscriptions and enjoying the night. It was simple and breathtaking, and I was with a beautiful person who I looked forward to spending more impulsive moments with during this season of my life.

Chapter Eight

Didn't Know Who I Am

Didn't Know Who I Am

You didn't know who I am, You didn't remember my name.
You didn't look at me, My visit wasn't the same.
You didn't remember my touch; You didn't know my voice.
My face did not look familiar, My words were not your choice.
You raised me from a child, Taught me "yes sir and yes ma'am".
So, it hurts me each day to know, You don't know who I am.
But you taught me about a Savior, Who would never leave me alone.
Who knows the pain you can't see, Who's with me wherever I roam.
So, it may not be the same, My relationship with you.
But I am living the life you taught me, Christian instructions in what I should do.
For you may not remember me naturally, Your child with the birthmark of a ham.
But spiritually you know your girly, And I know you know who I am.
Spirit Inspired™ Didn't Know Who I Am© by Kay Henley

Kayla

June 2020: It's Been One Year

My father died on June 4, 1995, from Alzheimer's complications. My mother died on June 11, 2019, from an infection incurred due to her decades-long battle with rheumatoid arthritis. I remember both daily, and I remember what was going on and where I was when they both passed. This was the first year without both of them. God blessed me with Myles, but being an only child still left me feeling lonely. I was determined not to let it get in my head, but it did.

Myles asked, "What are we doing to remember your mother?"

"Their graves are in Norfolk, but I know they are with me. So, I think I will just stay here and remember them." I replied.

"Let's go to Norfolk. I know they are not there, but it may help you on this day to remember them."

Norfolk, here we come! Norfolk is a three-hour drive from DC (with no traffic). I called my uncle and the ladies who had taken care of my mother. We met at the cemetery, which was not far from my parents' home.

When my father passed, I bought a plot for both, but the headstone only had his name on it. I purchased a new headstone, double-sided, with both of their names. I have always believed, as stated in 2 Corinthians 5:8 (NKJV): "We are confident, yes, well pleased rather to be absent from the body and to be present with the Lord."

My soul was at peace because I knew my parents were with my Lord and Savior.

We met at the cemetery. I pulled some weeds from the plot. We laid flowers and each had a moment of peace at the grave site. We left the site and went about our day. My parents were at peace, and they had given me a blessed life. I realized, though, that the numbness in me was still real even though I could see that God was moving in and blessing my life. Myles saw my heart that day and his compassion was beyond what I needed.

Chapter Nine

I Love You Even More

I Love You Even More
I love you even more today,
Than I did yesterday.
I love you for the man you were,
And the man you are today.
I love the spirit you share with others,
And the passion for God in your heart.
The love of Him and His Son,
It is a spiritual walking art.
You have touched my soul like no one else,
And I know this love is God's way.
Thank you for listening to Him for our path,
I love you even more each day.
Spirit Inspired™ I Love You Even More© by Kay Henley

Kayla

June 2020: "So, You Think You Want to Get Married?"

Our church recommends any members who want to be married at the church or by one of the ministers must complete two premarital classes. The recommendation was not an option for us since we were taking the class. I needed to attend because I had never been married before and Myles needed a refresher.

Myles had been friends for decades with the couple who wrote the book and course curriculum and also taught the class. I did not know them, and in my mind, I am sure they were thinking what A LOT of people at the church were thinking: *Who is she? Where did she come from? How did she get him?* Given that I was completely walking in faith, whether I knew it at the time or not, thoughts, looks, and comments did not affect me; this was totally of God.

We decided to take the condensed weekend class in June, which gave us three months to get to know each other even more. I did not spend the time planning a wedding because we had not set a date. Plus, the class instructors highly recommended that you do not plan the wedding because, after all, the class is called "So you THINK you want to get married."

We wanted to be clear and certain about this decision. I asked him about his expectations of me as a wife and of me in a relationship with his children (because I was NOT going to be a stepmother because they were grown). I also asked about financial expectations (i.e., who and how the finances would be handled) and where we would live (his house was larger, and he had no mortgage; I had a townhome).

We talked about sexual expectations, relationships with family, friends, church ministry service, my sorority activities, his golf buddies—all relationships and personal interactions. We even discussed toilet paper—over or under—and we agreed we are an under house; deal with it. We were proactive in managing expectations.

We read Gary Chapman's *The 5 Love Languages* on how to communicate with your spouse. I learned that both Myles and I are combinations. Myles's love languages were physical touch and quality time, which explained why he always wanted to hold my hand or sit close to me. I was not used to that, so it was an adjustment. On the other hand, my love languages were quality time and acts of service. We overlapped in quality time, and Myles had a heart for service at home and especially at church. Acts of service was interesting because Myles liked to do almost everything around the house. He told me he wanted to cook dinner, preferred washing the dishes (I am team dishwasher), and do all the outside yard work.

I learned that doing yard work was his fellowship time with God. He used the time to memorize scripture and pray. He told me that we could hire a service to clean the house since it was three levels (did I say he was a blessing or what?!). I insisted on doing the laundry, though. Marriage assignments were done! We successfully completed the weekend class!

Myles

June 2020: Becoming One

One of the requests I had of Kayla was for us to complete a premarital class taught by one of my good friends and his wife. The class offered the opportunity to see beyond the physical attributes in each other and address real-life issues from a biblical perspective. It also gave us an opportunity to state marital expectations and accommodations.

The class allowed me to see that Kayla would be willing to compromise in this relationship. Also, I told Kayla during the class that she did not have to work. Not only because I was financially set but because I wanted to spend as much time as I could with her during this season in my life.

This class allowed me to see a woman who is not only beautiful outside but also beautiful inside. I am definitely in love with all of her. We successfully completed the class, and now it was time to pick out the rings. I decided in my mind that she could have whatever she desired.

Kayla

June 2020: First Thing First – The Ring

A few weeks after completing the class, we shopped for our rings. I had no clue what I wanted. I was not one of those women who had planned her wedding all her life. I honestly had not thought about it. I wanted something that reflected us and our beliefs. The moment I saw it, I knew that was what I wanted—a three-stone ring. The three-stone engagement ring means:

-the past, present, and future of a relationship

-the trinity of friendship, love, and fidelity

-the Holy Trinity in Christianity

That ring truly represented us. I selected the ring. I was conscientious of a budget and thought one carat would be fine, but Myles upgraded it to three carats. I also chose two rings for him—his wedding ring and a friendship ring, just because. The rings were chosen, and it was now time to tell people and plan a wedding.

Myles just had two requests for the wedding, which seemed simple enough.

1. Make it this year

2. I want you to have a wedding.

Wow...this man is it!

Myles

June 2020: Setting the Date/Looking for Locations

I will admit that I do not like living alone. I had been married for over forty years and was not used to being by myself. At the same time, I was not getting married just to have a wife. Kayla met the requirements, so I told her that I did not want to wait a year to get married.

After the marriage class, we knew what was expected of us, from God and from each other. We set the date and looked for locations. Hey—I am not getting any younger, and plus, I was abiding by the "no kiss" rule. I was ready for this marriage for multiple reasons, *if you know what I mean.*

Kayla

June 2020: Setting the Date/Looking for Locations

Wynter, my friend and sorority sister told me, "Kayla, don't be one of those brides who goes back to your hometown church to get married. Your family is not there, and we are going through a pandemic."

That message was clear, and she had a good point. I had been thinking that it would be cool to get married in the church my parents got married in, but she was right: they are both dead, and most of the family and friends from my hometown and my church no longer lived in my hometown.

Myles and I decided to have the ceremony in our current living area.

We spent two June weekends checking out venues in Virginia and Maryland. When we arrived at the Springfield Manor Winery Distillery in Thurmont, Maryland, I knew it was the perfect place.

The winery was built in 1775 by James Johnson, one of the founders of the Catoctin Furnace, which produced pig iron, an essential element for ammunition and construction. During most of the 18th and early 19th century, workers at the furnace were enslaved African Americans. The property was converted in 2004 and has a lavender field in the front of the property, a distillery and winery on one side, and a bed and breakfast venue with an outdoor wedding venue.

The most beautiful part is that the outdoor chapel's backdrop is the Catoctin Mountains. They are on the easternmost mountain ridge of the Blue Ridge Mountains, which are a part of the Appalachian Mountains range.5 I am sure my African ancestors who worked there were proud that they could now see a place where they were once enslaved now being used for a good purpose.

God blessed me with the vision at that moment. The wedding would be in October, a year after our TRUE first meeting. I wanted to have the wedding on Saturday—10/10/2020, but EVERYONE else seemed to also want that date.

Seriously, why is everyone getting married on the date that I wanted during a pandemic?!

I prayed about it and God brought two things to my attention. First, it was the pandemic; no one was really working, and who said you had to get married on Saturday? Secondly, weddings during the week are cheaper (and Myles is blessed to marry a sparely frugal woman—meaning, fugal when it was not going in my pocket).

We spoke with the venue, prayed about it, and set the date: Wednesday, 10/21/2020. Why 10/21? It was the numeric number of my home address. The date worked perfectly for us and the venue.

It was now late June, and I needed to plan a wedding in four months... during a pandemic! Challenge accepted.

The Magic Words

Myles and I were talking about our future one day and revisiting what we learned from the class.

"What do you plan to do about your job?" he asked.

I took a moment to ponder. "What do you mean?"

"I know you probably love working, and you're close to retirement, but please know that you do not have to work once we get married."

Wow, I told myself, *hold your composure, think about your words, breathe.* "Could you please repeat that?"

"I don't want you to feel like you have to work once we get married. We are good. If you want to retire, you can. I GOT YOU."

I thought first, Wow, my old school husband is going to take care of his wife... Breathe. "Okay. Let me think about that," I said.

I had never seriously thought about when I was going to retire. I knew I was eligible next year, but I had not given it much thought. Then again, I was eligible now, thanks to the great benefits of my job. I could have walked out two years ago, but I was still in the mindset of "*I have to take care of my mother. I have to take care of me.*" Now that my mother was gone, I could consider the possibility.

Myles further clarified his position and stated, "I only request that you pay off all your debt before we get married. I can help you if you like. I do not want to go into the marriage with any debt. I am debt-free."

Okay, third, WOW! That was nothing but a word! I had freed up some cash before my mother passed, and it came in handy, not only for her funeral but also for some other financial issues after her death. I only had a car note and some credit card debt.

"Consider it done," I said. "But I will get back to you regarding retirement. I need to pray more about that one."

I had been working at one job or another since I was sixteen years old. I had been at my current job in various positions over thirty years. After nearly forty-three years in the workforce, I did not know what not working looked like.

I called my recently retired, all-wise and knowing, corporate mentor, Sophia, the next day. Sophia is awesome. She walks in her faith and is compassionate, strategic, and humble all at the same time. She was not only my mentor but also my carpool companion for over seven years, and we had a blast riding to work every day. She was my friend, counselor, and confidant. We talked about everything, and we always got to the point. So, I called her for advice as usual.

"Hi, Sophia, I am getting married," I exclaimed.

"Congratulations!" The joy in her voice was palpable.

"Myles said I don't have to work. What does that look like? I took all the retirement seminars the corporation offered, but I still cannot tell if I have enough money to retire," I said, sharing my concerns.

"You have enough, and most importantly, God got you because he brought Myles into your life for such a time as this. Most importantly, Myles wants someone to share his life with during this season and God gave you this season for all you have been through in your life while taking care of your mother. You honored your mother, and now God is giving you the desires of your heart. Go enjoy life… retire. You have enough," Sophia said.

She said all of that without having met Myles. Walking wisdom… and everyone should have a Sophia.

Chapter Ten

At Peace

At Peace
I've found that quiet place,
Where no one else can be.
But me and my Heavenly, loving Father,
Free to do and be as I please.
With joy I've found that happy place,
And a smile expresses it for me.
I don't have to go anywhere at all,
Just stand still, listen, and be.
For that Peace is with me wherever I am,
And wherever I am it will be.
I've found that joy that comes from God,
And that Peace resides in me.
Spirit Inspired™ At Peace© by Kay Henley

Kayla

July 2020: Telling My Family, Friends, and Coworkers

I had not officially told my family, friends, and coworkers that I was getting married and had set a date. It was time to do it.

Family: I called my uncle and my cousins, and they were all very happy for me. I asked my uncle, my mother's brother, to walk me down the aisle, and he readily agreed. Then I asked my cousin from Atlanta to be my matron of honor, and she also agreed. She has two daughters—my hearts—and I asked them to be my ushers. They were beyond excited. My young Richmond cousin informed me that he was going to be an usher in my wedding, and I smiled and agreed.

I told the rest of my cousins that due to the pandemic, we had to limit in-person attendance, but we would be streaming the wedding. They were all cool with that.

Co-workers: The pandemic was still going on, and no solution had been found. It was a sad time, and I sometimes almost felt guilty for being so happy during that time. We teleworked, and on one day, I had two virtual meetings that provided me the opportunity to share my happiness with everyone.

During a virtual meeting with my corporate team, I shared that I was getting married. They were all very happy for me, especially knowing that my mother had passed a year ago. They were congratulating me, asking for details, such as:

Who is he? Where does he work? How did you meet him?

Where are you going to live? Does he have a brother?

When my coworkers asked when I was getting married, I lit up. "When are you getting married?"

"I am getting married on Wednesday, October 21 at 3 pm in Frederick, Maryland. By the way, I am retiring on Friday, October 16," I said.

Silence. Crickets.

The cheers and celebration evaporated like ice on a hot day. More silence.

"Well, you should have begun with 'I am retiring on October 16,'" stated one of the directors.

It set in like a ton of rocks. I was going to leave them. Everyone eventually left the room. The celebration ended, And I was okay with that. Plus, I had more work to do.

Next, I had to tell my contracting team. I was a technical project manager of a major project for over two years. I had been blessed to have selected a field staff to assist me on the project. Melody brought institutional knowledge to the technical project. She was beyond an asset to me during the season when my mother was transitioning, and the team of young, think-outside-the-box contractors was awesome.

I notified Melody and the contracting team the same way I informed my corporate coworkers. While they were happy for me, they were sad I would no longer be on the project. They were more than my contractors; this group was like family. After the shock wore off, we got back to work. I started sharing with my friends and especially my sorority sisters, both from college and

alumnae chapters. Everyone was beyond happy for me. I called my two close friends, Teresa and Brenda, via a conference call.

"Hi Ladies. Thanks for taking my call. I hope all is well with you both."

"Girl, why are you making this sound like a business meeting? I am retired." Teresa quipped.

Brenda chimed in, "Yeah, what's up?"

"Well, it's official. I am getting married," I said.

They responded at the same time, "Awesome, congratulations!"

"This is great! So, Teresa and I are going to be bridesmaids. How many bridesmaids are you going to have? Who is going to be the matron of honor? What are your colors?" asked Brenda without taking a breath.

Bridesmaids? Matron of honor? Colors? And did I ask them to be my bridesmaids?

They've always had my back, so they knew they'd be in the wedding.

"Okay. Both of you, and definitely Myles's daughter, and my cousin, Kyra.

"Kayla, What about your sorority sisters?" Teresa asked.

"I love them all, but I do not want a big wedding due to COVID."

Teresa commented in a surprising but excited tone, "You are getting married this year?

Why?" Teresa said as she laughed. "You pregnant?"

I giggled and said, "No. Myles said he didn't want to wait. We completed the premarital class several weeks ago, so we decided to get married this year. We are not getting any younger."

Teresa countered, "What about COVID?"

"COVID is not invited. Also, we are having an outside wedding with a spacious inside

reception," I said.

"When? Where?" Teresa asked.

"Wednesday, October 21, in Frederick, Maryland."

"You are having an outside wedding in Maryland? In late October? In the middle of the week?" Brenda asked.

"Yes, yes, and yes," I said.

There was a slight pause before they said, "Okay."

I really had not thought about the wedding plans. I wasn't allowed to do so prior to completing the premarital class.

I put on my project manager hat and went to work because this was going to be a PANDEMIC COVID wedding! God, Myles and I got this!

- Set a budget
- Schedule a meeting with my bridesmaids
- Ask Myles to select groomsmen
- Decide on colors
- Create a guest list (we had decided to limit it to 50)
- Find a videographer
- Find a photographer
- Find a florist
- Find a singer
- Select songs
- Do the program
- Create invitations
- Select table covers and centerpieces

I needed a caterer for a cake. A wedding cake. Yes. That hit an emotional nerve. My mother had given me the topper from her wedding cake. For decades, I had kept it in a box at the top of my closet. They had been married forty years before my father passed. They were married on June 2, 1957. The cake topper was more than sixty-three years old and in good condition. I pulled it out of my closet, and whoever the caterer was, they had to do some restoration with the cake topper.

It will be used on the wedding cake. Uhm. What else? Am I missing something? Right! Kayla, get a dress!

Myles

July – October 2020: Getting Ready for the Wedding

Over the next few months, Kayla was into the wedding details, and I was happy for her. I had been married before, so I understood how a woman got excited about planning a wedding.

Kayla and I created a wedding budget, and I let her take charge of planning the details. Kayla kept me informed on every aspect of the wedding plans and sought my advice. I appreciated her and was happy she included me in the decisions, but even more happy that she did not include me in the implementation of the details. She had her "girls" for that, and I was beyond pleased about it. I ordered my tuxedo, selected my shirt, shoes, and socks, and waited for my wedding day.

Kayla

July - August 2020: Finding A Dress... During the Pandemic

It was the first week in July, and there were still three and a half months left until the wedding. I had to shop for a wedding dress during the pandemic. While I was a consummate Amazon shopper, I was not going to buy my dress from there! I definitely wanted to try the dress on, but I had to find a store that was open during the height of the pandemic before there was a vaccine.

After searching online, I found a store that was open. God blessed me with Mary's Bridal Boutique in Annapolis, Maryland, a city not far from my home. I called the number listed on the website, and after two long days, I received a call back from Mary, the owner.

"Hi, Kayla, this is Mary from Mary's Bridal Boutique. I got your message. Yes, you can come in and try on a dress. You must wear a mask, and you must come by yourself."

"Okay, but I cannot bring even one person with me?" I asked. Mary said, "Unfortunately, no. Just you."

"Okay. When can I come in?"

"Next Wednesday, 4 pm," Mary said. "Don't forget, come by yourself."

"Okay. See you then."

Mary asked, "By the way, when is the wedding? Next year?" "It's not next year. It's this October, October 21," I replied.

There was a slight pause and she continued in disbelief. "You are having a wedding during the pandemic?"

"Yes," I said, ignoring her tone. "See you next Wednesday at 4 pm."

"Okay, but it will have to be something in the store. The turnaround time is too short,"

Mary replied.

"No problem." I had seen enough of Say Yes to the Dress, to understand the process.

I went back online to search for a dress and get some ideas on what I might want. It felt like a full-time job! Then the tears came. This was something I always wanted to do with the woman who wanted this just as much as me. Now, I cannot do it with my mother, any family, or friends. I felt alone and isolated again. God immediately reminded me, "I will never leave you nor forsake you" (Deuteronomy 31:8). There it was again: F.E.A.R. *False Evidence Appearing Real*. God set this up and would be with me through it all. I just needed to get past "me" because God would make this right. I continued searching Mary's inventory online because I knew God would help me find my dress, and I would get married in October.

It's coming together

It was the end of August. Everything was coming together. Myles and the groomsmen had ordered their tuxedos—*check*. The bridesmaids' online dresses had already arrived, which were more beautiful than the pictures—*check*. I had selected a dress and accessories and had a second fitting set for September—*check*. The caterer had scheduled a taste testing for September, and I had already spoken with the florist about flowers—*check*. I found a videographer and a photographer online, and we had a Zoom call to make sure they could work together—*check*.

My hometown pastor agreed to do the wedding and had recommended a young lady who was not only one of my mother's children in kindergarten but also a professional opera singer; she also committed—*check*. I found someone from my local church to make the wedding/cupcake and she said she would use the cake topper from my parents' wedding—*check*. My former neighbor, a DJ, agreed to play the music at the wedding—*check*. I found fall-colored centerpieces and tablecloths at a store called "At Home", and I had compiled a list of songs I wanted to be played before the wedding and performed at the wedding—*check*. I also used Etsy to create the program and online invitations. I was on budget, and I was very proud of myself, given I was still working full-time.

I just needed Myles's guest list to finish the process, so I called him.

"Hi, Future Husband."

"Hi, Babe."

"When you get a chance, can you please email me your guest list?" Myles said, "Sure, emailing it to you now, and it is in a spreadsheet as you requested."

"Thanks, Honey. I will call you later."

Myles emailed the list within five minutes (his life motto is "Don't put off tomorrow what you can do today"). We had agreed to a maximum of fifty guests due to COVID. We had also decided to rent the bed and breakfast on the property. The wedding was going to be outside, and dinner would be served inside a spacious reception room with open doors (if needed) for ventilation. As I reviewed his list, I noticed there were at least thirty people on the list.

What? Breathe, Kayla. I called him back.

"Hi, Myles, just being real, but haven't you been married before?"

Myles replied, "Yes, what's up?"

"We have a limit of 50 people on this list. You have 30. This is my first and only wedding.

Can we split this or at least make it 30 for me and 20 for you?"

Myles laughed and said, "A 30/20 split is fine, but I had already told one of the couples to save the date."

"We will make a waitlist. I am sure he and his wife will understand. Someone may cancel since we are having a "Pandemic Wedding." Thanks for understanding, Baby." I said as I breathed a sigh of relief. "By the way, who are you telling they cannot attend?"

"One of the elders of the church and his wife," he said.

I thought, *what the hockey sticks? What are they going to think of me? Breathe, Kayla. Myles got this, and they will understand because it is the pandemic.*

"Okay. Thanks, my love."

No one canceled. We had twenty on the waitlist. I guess the shock of me getting married was worth risking the possibility of catching COVID. Those who couldn't make it would see it on YouTube.

Myles

August 2020: The List

I was so excited about the wedding that I wanted to invite as many close family and friends within the church as possible. I had been attending my church for over 30 years and had established relationships with a good number of close brothers. They all supported me during the transition of my wife, and I wanted them to celebrate with me as I married the woman God prepared for me. If they could tolerate the risk of COVID, then so could we. When Kayla called about the list, I laughed. I knew she did not think it was funny, but I hoped she realized my excitement in inviting so many people came from how proud I was to be marrying her. I would have to deal with uninviting the elders.

Chapter Eleven

Give Her Strength

Give Her Strength

Father God, give her strength, to live her life your way.
Father God, give her peace To love you every day.
Jesus Christ, be with her, to guide her path through you.
Jesus Christ, talk with her, Tell her what to do.
My Lord and Savior, heal her, of any and all pain.
Provide her with your glory, show her the Christian's gain.
Holy Spirit, speak for her, let her voice be heard.
Holy Spirit through Jesus Christ, to God make known her words.
Father God, protect her,
For everything Christ's death meant.
Holy Spirit, speak to her, Father God - give me strength.
Spirit Inspired™ Give Her Strength© by Kay Henley

Kayla

September 2020: Two Months to Go

Things were being added to the wedding project. Myles and I learned in late August that I had to "governmentally" be married sixty days before our wedding for him to be on my healthcare plans. My good government job provided me with a great benefits plan.

Pastor Smith met us in the DMV for dinner and signed papers we needed to submit to the county government where we were married. I was also in the process of downsizing my day job, reassigning responsibilities and making sure everyone understood what I did.

Amazingly, I had trained two people to replace me, but they only paid me one salary. Such is life—they only miss you once you are gone or when you are leaving. I had five weeks to train two people, one of whom lived in Kansas. The assignment was done with a smile.

Two exciting things were happening this month: my bridal showers.

My first bridal shower was given by my college sorority sisters. It was an outside celebration around a fire pit at my line sister's home. It was a lingerie party, well planned and a lot of fun. My favorite part was seeing everyone (albeit in mask) for the first time during the pandemic. We spent three hours in person, fellowshipping, eating, and opening gifts. These were ten of my closest sorority sisters in person, with several others sending gifts.

My second bridal shower was virtual. Teresa, Brenda, Kyra, and Toni had been working on it for weeks. There were over fifty of my closest family and friends on the call. My bridesmaid, Brenda, had cautiously come over a few days before the shower (working around COVID) and arranged all the gifts in order with name tags on who donated what. It was a beautiful arrangement. The Zoom call began well... and then *"Me"* happened.

"Kayla, we are going to open with prayer for your marriage," said one of the bridesmaids. "Okay," I replied. I needed this and couldn't wait to open the presents, just like a kid at Christmas looking at all the gifts but not being able to touch them.

The bridesmaid added, "Kayla, we have over fifty of your loved ones on the phone, and of course, your future daughter-in-love is there with you to assist in opening the presents that everyone so nicely sent in for this occasion."

The agenda for the four-hour Zoom shower was as follows:

-30 minutes of introductions of who is on the Zoom call, how they met me, and how long they have known me.

-45 minutes for a game of "How well do you know Kayla?"

-A 15-minute break

-15 minutes for individual refreshments

-Another game for 45 minutes

-Open the over fifty presents

What the hallelujah (getting better with the cursing)? Four hours on a Zoom call? Do they not know me? Okay, Kayla, decrease you and increase the spirit that lives in you. You can do this. Deep sigh after the review of the agenda, I thought.

Everyone on the call introduced themselves and shared how they knew me. It was funny because my friends had told me in the past that I tend to compartmentalize my friends—they were correct.

This would never happen again. The comments took more than 30 minutes; more like 45 minutes. Then we played the game "How well do you know Kayla?" There were 25 questions.

Everyone was emailed the questions in advance and had to send them back prior to the shower thanks to those detailed bridesmaids.

What is Kayla's Favorite Color? *Most got it right.*

Where was Kayla born? *Most got it right.*

Who was her first boyfriend? *A few got it right.*

What was her first job? *Most got it right.*

What was her college major? *Several guests got it right.*

What is her favorite food? *Most got it right.*

Then came the question that changed everything: What is her favorite drink? The bridesmaids asked me first and I said, "Dirty chai tea latte." The online guests BLEW UP!

"Kayla, that is NOT your favorite drink!"

"That must be your COVID drink because that is wrong."

"Every Starbucks in a 20-mile radius of your home knows that is not your favorite drink! Girl, when you walk through the door, Starbucks starts making your drink!"

Sophia, my corporate mentor and friend, calmed the masses and said, "Okay, everyone. I got this. I carpooled with Kayla for over seven years. Her favorite drink is caramel macchiato.

Ignore her."

Isn't this my shower? I guess the game is not about me.

"Yes, caramel macchiato is correct," I said as I laughed. We have now been on the call for more than ninety minutes. I was not going to make it. "Can we take a break?"

A bridesmaid said, "Okay. We can take a fifteen-minute intermission."

"Ladies, you all may not know, but Kayla has a very short attention span. The meetings that she led at work were never more than one hour. If she had to attend one that is more than an hour, especially online, trust and know there is a Candy Crush game going on." Sophia paused. "Suggestion, since we have so many on the call and given the bride has a "child-like" attention span, why don't we open the gifts after the intermission."

She saved me again!

One of the bridesmaids stated in protest, "WHAT? But we have another game? Really?"

"Sophia, thank you. See, if we were in person and I understand we cannot because of COVID, this would not be an issue because we would be talking to one another. My attention span is short because I am sitting here watching a screen. So, yes! Let's come back after intermission so this "child" can open the gifts!" I said.

Remember that beautiful arrangement Brenda organized and set up? Destroyed!

I opened those gifts like a child on Christmas morning.

"This is from *(insert name)*. I love it. Thanks. Toni (onsite bridesmaid and future daughter-in-love), please hand me another gift."

This went on for another thirty minutes. When I say I destroyed the organized process, I opened those gifts so fast that one would have thought a hurricane hit the room. I did a great job, loved all my gifts, and was very proud of my gift-opening success. My bridesmaids were PISSED I did not follow the format, but the shower was over. They knew I loved them and appreciated all they did, but this was my one Bridezilla moment.

October 2020: 21 Days

It was October 1, and I was in my head. My mind was on the details of the wedding, which was all coming together, while at the same time trying to figure out how to close out twenty-nine years at my job. So much had happened during that time: my father had passed, I had traveled the country for my job with my friends, jumping in on many of the assignments, and some coworkers became friends. I was excited about moving forward, but this would be the first time since I was sixteen that I did not have a job.

I looked in the mirror and consulted with my favorite people: *Me, Myself, and I*. My mind began to race with one thought after the next. *Well, I am tired of working. Same stuff every day, whether remotely or in-person.*

Look, they are replacing you with two people. They never appreciated you, and nothing is going to change here. NEXT. The pay is great, and you know this stuff. Your contractors love you, and the rest of your coworkers have learned to tolerate you. Also, although it seems like you have enough to retire, you don't know that for sure. You are going to have to change your hairstyle because if you retire, "your husband" is not going to let you get your hair done every week. Why should he? You don't have to go anywhere every day! You are going to be bored, no matter how much you planned, as that retirement consultant suggested. Look, this is not about us. This is a blessing from God, and it is good. You have always been afraid to step out on faith. Well, this is the faith of your mother's prayer and your prayers. God got us and we got this! We are moving forward.

I knew this type of thinking would do me no good, so I walked away from the mirror, got down on my knees, and prayed, *God, thank you for being my God and giving me this life. Thank you for ignoring my fears. Thank you for answering my mother's request and my prayer. Thank you for the Holy Spirit that lives in me and that I will definitely be relying on through my fears over the next 21 days. Thank you for Myles, who is perfect for this season in my life. You are truly an awesome God, and I can never thank you enough for all you have done for me. In Jesus' Name. Amen.*

As a super planner, I made a list of all the tasks I had to do before the wedding.

I set my retirement date as Friday, October 16, five days before my wedding.

- Clean out my office *(check)*

- Turn in my laptop *(check)*

- Turn in all my other electronic security stuff and badges *(check)*

- Oh yeah—go to my virtual retirement celebration!

- Deia, one of my work besties, offered to give me a virtual retirement celebration.

"Hey girl, I got this thing, but one question: Is there anyone you would like to speak at your retirement celebration?" Deia called and asked.

"All of my managers—prior and current." Shocked, she said, "Really? Wow! Okay."

I may have been a challenging employee on occasions, questioning assignments and challenging regulations and rules; with that said, though, all of my managers appreciated my drive and passion for my work ethics. I had no doubt it was going to be a positive celebration.

I gave Deia their names and all my managers stepped up to the plate. It was so awesome to *hear* all the nice things they had to say. I finally felt appreciated but realized I was already appreciated—by God.

Back to the wedding with three days to go!

- My dress and shoes *(check)*

- Reception decoration *(check)*

- Bridesmaids all set *(check -dresses came in from Hong Kong in two months)*

- Groomsmen all set *(check)*

- Groom all set *(check)*

Every "T" was crossed and every "I" was dotted except one thing—what was I going to do with my hair!?! It was the pandemic. Nothing was open… but God.

I was able to get an appointment with a braid stylist two days before my wedding. They did an awesome job. Reflecting back on my first of the month prayer—no fear, total trust in God for this wedding but most importantly for the marriage.

Chapter Twelve

You and I

"Here we are on earth together it's You and I, God has made us fall in love it's true,
I've really found someone like you. Will it stay, the love you feel for me,
Will it say that you will be by my side to see me through,
Until my life is through,
Well in my mind, we can conquer the world, In love, You, and I, You and I,
You and I."
"You and I" by Stevie Wonder©

Kayla

Wedding Day

We were married at that bed and breakfast winery in the mountains of Maryland. I had prayed that God would paint the mountains in autumn colors (and He did), that it would not rain (and it didn't), and that it would be a beautiful, warm, autumn day (and it was—unusually warm for the Maryland mountainside on October 21).

Myles rented the entire bed and breakfast house for our family and friends for two days.

At 11 am (I was already awake), my bridesmaids came to my room so we could fellowship, pray, and get dressed.

Teresa exclaimed, "It's your wedding day! Let's get it going! How are you doing?" Good question. I really didn't know, but I said, "Great! Ready for this day."

The Caterers

While driving up to the venue, Anne said to her husband John, "Honey, this is a beautiful day for a wedding. It's not too hot and not too cold. I pray Myles and Kayla love the cake and cupcakes. Her parents' cake topper fit perfectly. Just think—it is more than 60 years old, and she preserved it well."

With a smile, John responded, "Indeed, Honey. I am sure she will love everything. I did a taste test, and I approve. Definitely a beautiful day; not a cloud in the sky."

Anne glanced up and said excitedly, "John, LOOK! The sky is clear except for those clouds ahead." As they approached the venue, she continued. "Honey, the clouds formed a cross in the sky—over her venue! There is nothing else in the sky but the cross. Wow! Look at God!"

"Wow! Anne, this wedding is truly blessed," John said.

Myles

October 21, 2020: Wedding Ready

I woke up at 6 am that day to pray, eat, and reflect. I prayed for our upcoming nuptials. I prayed for her health, and I prayed for my health. I thanked God for the lessons I learned from my prior marriage. I prayed to God to be the best husband I could be for Kayla.

After breakfast, I got ready for the wedding. It was 11 am, and the wedding was not until 3 pm. Pictures were scheduled to be taken at 1 pm, but I just wanted to be ready and outside with God at this beautiful venue. I walked the venue grounds, visited family and friends who had arrived early, and waited for my bride.

Kayla

October 21, 2020: Wedding Ready

Before the wedding, my mind was consumed with thoughts of my parents and all the things I learned in the premarital class. I couldn't help but wonder if I could live up to Myles's and God's expectations.

I wanted to go outside and walk the beautiful grounds. I felt God was calling me to do that, but instead, I just gazed out the window. I could not believe God had blessed me this way, exactly like I prayed for and in His perfect time—at the perfect time in my life. At that moment, though, while gazing out the window, I had an unbelievable peace come over me. God was with me.

"Ladies, I am ready! Toni will do our makeup, Pastor Smith will come in for prayer, and the photographer will then take our pictures. Please let my Uncle know I am ready."

Final Heavenly Conversation

The Trinity: Peter, see, We told you it would all come together.

Peter: Yes! Praise God. This has answered Rosa's prayers. I see she has asked all ancestral spirits to come to the wedding. They look great!

Conclusion

Kayla

I believe my mother knew she was dying several weeks before she passed. She started asking me questions like, *"Are you going to sell or rent the house after I die?"* In my typical sarcastic response, I looked at her and said, "That is something you will not have to worry about when you are dead, right?" (Typical me to deflect).

One of her other comments, and there were many I did not emotionally receive, was, "I guess I will not see you get married." Ouch! I had no comment and couldn't look at her, but in my mind, I didn't think it would happen at my age.

On October 21, 2020, a year, four months, and two days after my mother passed, I got married! Only God! I know it was her final prayer, and I know it was her petition when she arrived in Heaven (augmented in my mind, with her famous hot rolls). I know my mother and father, a host of ancestors and friends were all dressed, seated, and watching the wedding. I know they all saw me marry my best friend. God blessed us with the desires of a mother and her daughter's heart at the perfect time: *a husband, someone so right for me.*

You Will See Me Get Married

I know you will see me get married;

It was the desire of both of our hearts.

That your only child would be happy,

Not alone when we are apart.

I know you will be watching over me,

It's what you did all of your life.

Through prayers and petitions to our Lord and Savior,

That this spirit would one day be a wife.

I know you are picking out what to wear,

For nothing can be varied.

With ancestors and all your friends looking on,

I know you will see me get married.

Spirit Inspired™ You Will See Me Get Married© By Kay Henley-Richardson

"Delight yourself in the Lord, and He will give you the desires of your heart."

Psalm 37:4

References

1. https://godwinks.com/pages/about-whats-a-godwink

2. The Power of Abundant Life. Pastor John K. Jenkins, Jr. December 2019.

3. "Washington Has a Shortage of Single Educated Men. Could Amazon Fix That?" Schweitzer, Ally. December 10, 2019. WAMU 88.5

4 Maryland Gender Ratios

5 Catoctin Mountain Park. https://www.nps.gov/cato/index.htm

References

About the Author

Kay Henley-Richardson is an accomplished poet. Her poems were turned into inspirational greeting cards, and produced in a unique prayer cards gift box, by Books are Fun in 2005. The gift box was distributed in the US and Canada. Kay continues to write poetry having self-published several cards, posters, and bookmarks sold at various trade shows. She enjoys serving at her church, in her sorority, and on several non-profit Boards. Kay finds contentment in writing, traveling, and spending time with family and friends.

Printed in the USA
CPSIA information can be obtained
at www.ICGtesting.com
CBHW070710230624
10444CB00014BA/959